T0266740

Then & Now

Then & Now

The World's Center
and the Soul's Demesne

EVA BRANN

PAUL DRY BOOKS
Philadelphia   2015

First Paul Dry Books Edition, 2015

Paul Dry Books, Inc.
Philadelphia, Pennsylvania
www.pauldrybooks.com

A version of "Imaginative Conservatism" first appeared on
The Imaginative Conservative, an online journal.

Printed in the United States of America

Library of Congress Cataloging-in-Publication Data

Brann, Eva T. H.
  Then & now : the world's center and the soul's demesne /
Eva Brann.
     pages cm
  ISBN 978-1-58988-101-3 (paperback)
 1. Herodotus. History. 2. Herodotus—Criticism and
interpretation. 3. Greece—History—To 146 B.C.
4. Greece—History—Persian Wars, 500–449 B.C.
5. Iran—History—To 640. 6. Greece—Relations—Iran.
7. Iran—Relations—Greece. 8. Conservatism—
Philosophy. 9. Imagination (Philosophy) 10. Disposition
(Philosophy) I. Title. II. Title: Then and now.
  PA4004.B727 2015
  938.007202—dc23
                                             2015013494

Contents

Then & Now

Comprehended by Herodotus

HOW THE GREEK CENTER IS DEFINED
BY THE BARBARIAN PERIPHERY

You would have to be pretty flat-souled not to be enchanted by Herodotus's "history," sometimes called *The Persian Wars*. Herodotus's own title seems to have been *The Inquiry* (*historie* in his Ionic dialect, *historia* in Attic Greek). You might indeed be put off by some of the confident detail of his reports, which are patent incredibilities fed to his credulous inquiries—for example, Greece was invaded by a Persian force totaling precisely 5,283,220 people (VII 184 ff.)—this great war demanded implausible numerosity. Or you might shake your head at the simple artlessness of his tales, which

This essay is dedicated, with warm thanks, to the Summer Classics Seminar on The Persian Wars *(St. John's College, Santa Fe, N.M, 2013). It lived up to its literal meaning, "seed-bed," by sprouting the ideas here harvested. Particular thanks to seminar member Mary Jane Myers for supplying me with Plutarch's "The Malice of Herodotus" and Cavafy's poem "Waiting for the*

are plainly priestly confabulations elicited by his press-ing questions. For example, Helen was never at Troy but sat out the first great war between Greeks and Barbar-ians in Memphis, Egypt—the priests told Herodotus that this information came from her cuckolded husband, Menelaus himself (II 113 ff.); this famous Trojan expedi-tion required, Herodotus thinks, nullification.

Herodotus's—only occasional—want of informational accuracy or narrative credibility might make us, make any reader, conceive the flat-footed notion that his "his-tory" is a miscellany of marvels, a collection of curi-osities, an anthology of digressions and excursions, delivered with beguilingly naïve candor in his suave, though by no means easy, Ionian Greek, which it would take a rare combination of Greek learning and English ear to reproduce in translation.

We would be wrong. Candid directness and naïve receptivity seem to me to be intellectual virtues that are more conducive to subtlety and depth than crafty obliqueness and obtuse sophistication. Behind Herodo-tus's wide-eyed sight-seeing and absorbent story-telling there is, I hope to begin to show, a deep-intentioned *schema*. By this term I mean a quasi-pictorial under-standing (detailed below) that bestows overall cohe-

---

Barbarians," and to my colleague Frank Pagano for his lectures on Herodotus.

The Landmark Herodotus: The Histories, *edited by Robert B. Strassler, is invaluable for this sort of general meditation by reason of its copious apparatus: dated outlines, marginal synop-ses, detailed maps, and a meticulous index. Where a literal trans-lation was needed, I have reworked the Landmark text.*

sion on the whole "showing-forth" (*apodexis*, I 1), as he styles his work and, moreover, informs each of his 1534 paragraphs with referential significance—well, perhaps not every one, since a relaxed receptivity, eschewing a system, that is, a remainderless integration of every detail, is also his way.

I call this way *schematic* as opposed to *theoretical*,[1] and it seems to me to fit perfectly the study that Herodotus is bringing into being in his "history." I have kept this word in quotation marks, but as soon as I have explicated the first paragraph of his work, the *History* will seem to be the right title, liberated from raised-eyebrow quotes: *The History*, by Herodotus of Halicarnassus, composed between the 450s and 420s B.C.E.[2] To me, there is a poignancy in witnessing the joyous dawn of a discipline that will come to be thought of as a resurrection—or laying to rest—of the past, one constrained by professional protocols of research.

A BEING CAN BE apprehended by its inner nature, its essence, or comprehended by its outer limits, its borderlands, and so by direction or indirection. Direct definition goes straight to the center of things; indirect definition achieves understanding by surrounding the object with girdling oppositions. It allows what the thing is to coalesce out of what it is not.

---

1. "Theoretical" in the modern sense of "conceptual." The original ancient meaning of *theoria*, "beholding," "viewing," as by a spectator, fits him very well.

2. All dates are B.C.E., unless otherwise noted.

In the following presentation I will try out a claim,
or a first approximation to a claim, that Herodotus's
inquiry follows a schema of such oblique delineations,
the largest of which is literally spatial—the geograph-
ical schema in which the Barbarian nations of the inhabited world surround Greece in a sweeping circuit
physically and circumscribe the character of the Hellenes (the name of the Greeks taken as a nation) by various antitheses. And, drawing more inward within the
circuit, the inquiry centers in on Athens as the pivot of
the human world, edged into that innermost position by
its one, particular, fraternal antagonist, Sparta. Sparta,
by its very explicit regulatedness, appears to me to bring
out Athens' more elusive essence, which is, let me say it
right now, its *freedom*. The centering is finally concen-
trated in individuals, two opposite yet typical Spartans,
Leonidas and Pausanias, and their common antithesis,
Themistocles. The illuminating schema is, then, that of
concentric bands, partly spatial, partly notional, partly
personal, each of which defines its inner neighbor by its
own otherness.

Thucydides, whose *Peloponnesian War* has a far
more chronological, in fact an annalistic (year-by-year),
structure, recounts the aftermath of the Asian invasion, beginning with the "fifty-years" period (*pentekon-
taetia*), during which Athens herself, the triumphant
prime opponent of the Persian empire, acquires an oppressive empire by means of the Delian League, formed
originally by her and her Greek allies to entrust her
with the further defense of Greece against the defeated
but undeterred Persians. As a devastating postscript to

Athens' dominance, a civil war between the two quint-essentially Greek cities ensues. Now—and this is to my point—Thucydides explicitly contrasts the ethnicities of Athens and Sparta in a set speech by those inveterate bystanders, the Corinthians (Thucydides 1 70). But he also offers, in the most famous of all his authentically in-vented speeches (as he himself might put it I 22), namely, Pericles' Funeral Oration (II 35 ff.), a purely positive, indeed a glowing portrait of Athens' essence. Not so Herodotus, though the city shone for him, if anything, more purely. He composes no such summary encomium, no analytic description of what one might call Attic hel-lenicity. I take that absence to be something like a cor-roboration of the claim that he pinpoints by indirection, by means of otherness—implicitly.

Of course, one might say that the Athens of which Thucydides writes was in fact more splendid than that of Herodotus, having, in the two generations between 479 (the end of the Persian invasion) and 431 (the time of the Funeral Speech), increased both her prosperity and her peril by the acquisition of that empire (Thucydides I 97). To Thucydides, the Athens of Salamis is not, as it is to Herodotus, the true victor of the Persian War by reason of her unselfish devotion to the Greek nation and to her own freedom; it is rather Sparta, who commanded by virtue of her greater power—an implicit but unmis-takable, even spectacular, reversal of his predecessor's judgment (I 18). But my faith is in "Herodotus of Hali-carnassus," not because he lived closer to the event, but precisely because, as a man from the margins, he evalu-ates the earlier city as a cosmopolitan, from the outside in, delineated by its Barbarian periphery, while "Athenian Thucydides" (*Thoukydides Athenaios* I 1) sees her past locally, first as a participant general, and later as an exile with the Peloponnesians (IV 104, V 26).

Herodotus does have a supply of more direct explanatory devices—"aetiological" stories (*aitios*: "causal") and event-chronologies. But his underlying mode is, I will try to show, implicit definition by showing forth otherness.

That is a way of shaping his inquiry, though I wouldn't call it a method. It involves getting large aggregate effects by individual micro-motivations. Indeed, that way almost defines Herodotus's history. *Historia*, "inquiry," is normally used of careful, detailed observation, be it of human actions or of nature (for example, by Plato, *Phaedo* 96a; the pursuit of universals, on the other hand, he calls *zetesis*, "search," *Meno* 80e). A certain sort of modern treatment of affairs abounds in sweeping, incantatory references to "social," "political," "economic," or "religious" causes, as if the mere terms were explanatory. Herodotus has no such theoretical rubrics, but he offers dreams, oracles, tales, and reports by the score.

For example, a dream is behind the crucial passage of the kingship from the relatively regional Medes to the expansive Persians (I 108); dreams are, Herodotus quotes a wise Persian as saying, about what we were thinking of by day (VII 16). An ambiguous oracle, providentially interpreted by Themistocles, causes the Athenians to begin to build themselves a navy, which turns out to be their salvation (III 143). A tale allows Herodotus to let Greek opinion be reflected from Asian venues (his "Asia" is our Asia Minor, IV 38). The Lydian King, Croesus, the first Asian we hear of to be in regular communication with Greeks, elicits from his Athenian visitor, Solon, the founder of Athens' democracy, a story exemplifying a notion of happiness opposed to his own belief in wealth as good fortune: Two youngsters, Cleobis and Biton, drag their mother's oxcart (her oxen not being back from the fields) to a distant festival. They arrive in time, take a nap, and die in their sleep (from heart attacks, I imagine), thus fulfilling their mother's prayer for them—to get the best thing a human being might have—which Solon interprets as short lives honored by excellence (I 131).[3] In another example of Asian mores reflected in a Greek's account, a causal story explains this king's lineage, which was instituted through a bedroom cabal occasioned by a woman's shame at being exhibited naked (I 7 ff.).

Herodotus reports such stories not always as *having happened* but rather as *being believed*—which does not obligate him to belief (VII 152). What people believe and tell about themselves, it scarcely needs saying, is a significant part of who they are—more illuminating than large-grained, unspecified explanatory concepts. Similarly, an exemplary individual, a being who in his own specificity expresses an ethnic type—an occurrence which is a fact of life and an enigma of philosophy—is more revealing than a conceptual abstraction. At least I

---

3. I have myself seen the hefty statues of these stalwart brothers at Delphi (archaic, 600, 7 ft., by Polymedes). They have the Egyptian look that art historians discern in archaic statuary.

think that this is Herodotus's warrant for his inquiry—whether he made it explicit to himself (it is not so in his work), I wouldn't know. However, he is known to have held recitations at Athens in mid-century, so how could he have escaped such questions? My point here is that it is not wide-eyed naiveté but thoughtful interest in the emergence of national character that is behind his storytelling.[4]

Part of our sense of Herodotus's unmodern credulity surely comes from his view of the gods, though there are two opposing opinions about his religiosity: he was a rationalizing skeptic and he believed what other Greeks believed. He had learned a lot about local religions, especially in Egypt, much more than he feels the need to tell, since "I believe that all people understand these things equally" (II 3). What I would like to express is his incredulous credulity, his ready receptivity to wonders that are marvelous without being believable. This disposition to marvel brings him close to his rival, Homer, one of whose frequent phrases is *thauma idesthai*, "a wonder to behold," used, for instance, in the *Odyssey*, of yarn being spun, of walls with palisades, of clothes and cloth (vi 306, vii 45, viii 366, xiii 108), that is, in

---

4. How a people's way comes into being, how the mutual reflection of individual and group works, is thus a problem close to the surface of the *History*. In my reading, Adam Smith, in the first section of his *Theory of Moral Sentiments* (1759), treats this question most ingeniously. He establishes a perfect circularity of individual and societal judgment, thus doing an end run around any grounding theory. So does Herodotus, who observes the schema and lets it speak for itself.

general of artifacts. So Herodotus is no systematic skeptic, but neither is he an easily-taken-in gawker.

In the case of the gods, he has a keen relish for their local guises, and even for their human-all-too-human priests and for the bribable or tricky—though sometimes wisely prescient—oracles. The Delphic Oracle in particular, which can be bought or pressured (V 62, VII 141), fascinates him with its cunning ambiguities (I 53, VII 141); he knew it to be the information center of the world.

What makes Herodotus more than a religious sight-seer is his conviction, attested above, that divinity is accessible to all humanity but that it assumes ethnic modes. He thinks the Egyptians were the first to differentiate the gods, and the Greeks learned it from them (I 49 ff.; Herodotus has no Greek priority-pride at all). But it was "only yesterday" that Hesiod and Homer "made up" or "rendered in poetry" (*poiesantes* can mean either) the gods' "surnames" (*eponymiai*), their births, honors, skills, and looks (II 53). Any chief god, be it Baal of the Babylonians or the Heavens of the Persians, is surnamed "Zeus" by Herodotus.

When students of comparative religion "identify" this ethnic god with that one, they do not usually feel obligated to muse on the opacity of the procedure. Do they mean that there actually exists one god who has different names in different locales? Do they mean that when a Greek arrives in Babylon he says, seeing a statue of Baal, "That's the one we call Zeus"—or the same when in Persia he is told about the sky-god? Does the secular student of comparative religion decide, by his own will, that two local gods (in neither of whom he believes) have similar features and so are identical? In other words, is the inquiry about what the locals loosely opine, or what the scholars reason out—or is it about the divine mode of multiple manifestations, which is surely what the Egyptian priests seriously mean when they say that Osiris *is* Dionysus (II 42)?[5]

For Herodotus it *is*, I think, about the last, the nature of the gods. He is a theological cosmopolitan who regards local appearances of divinity with respectful interest, and his own beautiful Olympians with reverence—that reverence, unburdened by agonies of belief, that gods receive who exact no protestations of faith or avowals of existence, but only the ritual proprieties. So Herodotus looks to a divinity universally known but locally manifested.

Consequently, he is somewhat double-tongued about matters connected with the gods. In his account, they no longer fight alongside men in battles, as they did for Homer. He is a tolerant skeptic in some cases: He himself may prefer the more rationalistic of two accounts—but lets anyone take up whichever account he finds persuasive (II 146). Sometimes he is a doubter with a light touch: The Marathon runner Philippides fell in with the god Pan, he reports, but adds "as he said" (VI 105–106). The untouched honey cake in a temple on the Athenian Acropolis signifies that Athena has abandoned the

5. The problem I am broaching is that of the secular study of divinity—non-fideistic theology. My sense is that this is not a problem in the *History*, because Herodotus indeed regards divinity as real.

place; it used to be consumed by a great snake "as if it existed." On the other hand, he reports without a raised eyebrow the immediate re-sprouting of Athena's sacred olive (olives are very slow-growing) after being burned in the Persian sacking of the goddess's sacred precinct (VII 41, 55). I think Herodotus thought that strange and wonderful things do happen and also that human imagination is itself marvelous. It is not necessary to be insistently flat-footed; that famous "willing suspension of disbelief" (Coleridge in the *Biographia Literaria*) is a poet's prerogative—but a "historian's" duty. I put the job title in quotation marks here because it will already be obvious that the *History* is as much anthropology as history in our sense,[6] although this first anthropologist is not one to go native with empathy, or patronizing with superiority, or coldly objective with strenuous science.

BUT AFTER THIS PRELIMINARY digression on Herodotus's simplicity, let's get back to his own prelude, his first paragraph. It is a riot of disjoining conjunctions and coupling antitheses, which invites close attention because it does not so much formulate as exemplify his way:

Herodotus of Halicarnassus: this is his *showing-forth* (*apodexis*) of his *inquiry* (*historias*) [undertaken] so that neither *what has come to be* (*ta genomena*) through [the agency of] human beings might *in time come to be extinct* (*en chronoi exitela genetai*), nor

6. Where anthropology includes sub-disciplines such as ethnography.

the *works, both great and wondrous (erga megala kai thaumasta), shown forth (apodechthenta)*, some by *Hellenes*, others by *Barbarians, might come to be glory-less (aklea genetai)*—both other matters and the *cause (aitia)* through which they went to war with each other.

I have rendered this first paragraph literally[7] so as to point up its compressions and iterations, counter-poisings and collections—a compendium, as I said, of Herodotus's approach; please believe that the Greek is handsome.

The work begins with the author and his city on the coastal edge of Asia Minor, where Persia meets Greater Greece. There is an implicit contrast with Homer's poetry in this piece of prose. I imagine that it was intended to be read as the opening of the only other work so far rivaling the two Homeric poems together in bulk.[8] Both epics begin with an *unnamed* poet's invocation of the Muse, but Herodotus *himself*, by name, is "showing forth" *his* inquiry, *his* display: He is an *author of exhibitions*.

Again, recall that Herodotus's word *historia* gave our "history" its name. For us, history in the primary sense is a done deal; the word applies only secondarily to a discipline devoted to research into the past, but primarily to that past itself, to deeds that have gone largely extinct and require rediscovery. Herodotus's *historia*

---

7. Though atticizing Herodotus's Ionian dialect.

8. At least as preserved for us.

is based on the verb *historein*, "to learn by inquiry," and preserves an original sense of activity, of questing research; the setting-forth of the findings is a derivative meaning, and the deeds themselves are not "history" but "what has come to be:" He is a *reporter of temporal realities*.

One more important point: Translators tend to pluralize *historia*: "The Histories." Herodotus has a singular; this is *one*, unified, inquiry: He is the *composer of a unity*.

To reiterate: Herodotus calls his *History* a "showing-forth." This "showing-forth" appears again, as a past participle modifying the works of both Greeks and Barbarians. Works have to show up before they are shown forth: Herodotus re-displays what has already been displayed in the world. (I am assuming, as an article of hermeneutic faith, that none of his locutions are unintentional.) These works, which "have come to be" by the agency of human beings (*anthropoi*; not only men, which would be *andres*), may come to be extinct by virtue of time and so come to be glory-less.

Herodotus is showing forth[9] real events in prose. Fictions are told in verse by Homer. His Achilles does likewise, as he sits in his tent willfully withdrawn from battle, singing of the glory of men (*Iliad* IX 189). The

9. *Apodexis*, a showing-forth, is sometimes understood to refer not to Herodotus's inquiry but merely to its public display, to his oral presentation of his work. But then, why use the same verb of the originating deeds? In fact, Herodotus is the unabashed shower-forth of "monuments" of greatness in Nietzsche's sense (*The Use and Abuse of History* II, 1874).

glory bestowed by poets, be they blind bards or inactive warriors, is everlasting, but the events displayed in a history are time-affected: humans bring things into being, time brings them to extinction. This fact assigns history its task, and it also casts over the *History* a dark shadow. It was still in the works around the third quarter of the fifth century, mostly at the height of Athens' glory, but on the brink of the slippery slope of a "descending curve" (Willa Cather's phrase for decline-in-success[10]). Extinction-in-time is what drives the Herodotean inquirer into the past and makes him a historian in that special sense, a delver into the past. But it also makes him a projector of the future. For this *historia* not only recalls wonders in the memorial aspect, but shows forth causes, in its aetiological, its explanatory, mode—in particular the cause (*aitia*) of the greatest of all wars hitherto, the Persian Wars. That stories of the remote past are causal, and thus explanatory of the near-present (these wars took place perhaps a half-century before the *History* was completed), is Herodotus's specifically "historical" assumption, which thereby differs from the poets' archetypal myth-telling. Poetry absorbs the fictional present into a-chronological, timeless time, in which, though declines and extinctions are foretold (e.g. *Iliad* IV 51 ff.), they are peripheral; Homer's heroic archetypes, both characters and events, are potentially present everywhere and always. Herodotus's stories, on the other hand, although perhaps partly fictions, are human-all-too-human in their individual particularity and spatio-

---

10. 1932 Preface to *The Song of the Lark*.

temporal specificity. Therefore, as they tell the causes of the Great War, so that war itself intimates a great destruction late in its century—which Herodotus discerns: the end of Athens' glory.

In fact, I think this inquiry is less concerned with causes than with greatness and/or wondrousness. The two terms are not completely convertible, it turns out. All "great" (*megala*) works—and in the *History*, *megala* often means "great" in the sense of "big," as well, for Herodotus loves, as I mentioned, large, if unlikely numbers—are to be marveled at, but many strange and wonderful things are very small, such as the tooth the "Medizing" (Persian-friendly) old former tyrant of Athens coughs up into the sands of Marathon, a loss he rightly interprets as signifying that wherever it fell, that was as much of Athens as he would ever repossess (VI 107). Here is wondrousness, but tiny.

So it is great *or* wondrous works that show forth. Not all of these bear directly on the great Persian wars of 490–479. There are "others," other wars, other actors; they too, however, deserve not to be glory-deprived, and, as I think, to play a role in delineating the center which the Barbarians—Herodotus does not here call them Persians—will briefly win and then forever lose.

And this is the primary antithesis of the *History* as set out in its prelude: Hellenes and Barbarians. As this historian's temporal causes explain actions, this ethnologist's local distinctions define characters; genealogy and geography, temporal lines and spatial schemata, together structure the *History*—against a background of marveling wonder.

Who are the Barbarians by and for themselves? To begin with, they are literally, that is, spatially, on the periphery of the inhabited world; they surround the Greeks, east, south, north, and west. Herodotus laughs at people—first, Homer—who picture Ocean (*okeanos*, "swift-flowing") as a circle drawn by a compass, flowing around the earth (IV 36), but a bit of the circular schema survives with him, as in maps he saw (V 49). The question is whether Greek centrality is a mere consequence of the explorers and mapmakers being Greeks or simply a fact of Greece's Mediterranean, that is, middle location or the natural product of a climatically favorable geography (III 106, I 142); anyone who was in Greece before pollution will recall that the diaphanous atmosphere and temperate air tend to transform sight into insight, turbidity into lucidity.

The Hellenes are defined as monolingual, as a nation of sovereign cities that all speak Greek. The Barbarians, seen from the inside out, are everybody else, more tribal than civic. The origin of "barbarian" was for the Greeks onomatopoetic, rendering the bar-bar-bar gabble of aliens; Herodotus himself speaks of barbarian twitter (II 57).[11] But people agree that "barbarian" is not normally derogatory for Herodotus; it simply means both non-Greek and polyglot.

Of course "Greek and Barbarian" is not a balanced opposition. A visitor to Athens in Plato's dialogue *The Statesman* points out that this accepted division of peo-

---

11. Alternatively, it was perhaps a Babylonian-Sumerian loan word: *barbaru*, "foreigner."

ples into Greeks and Barbarians is not good classifica-
tory practice (262 c–e), opposing, as it does, the few
Greeks against the many and multifarious others. But
then, Herodotus is applying not a philosophical method
of division but a historical topography of notions—an
ethnographic schema.

Herodotus respects and admires much about the Barbarian nations he has seen and reports, in satisfyingly
gruesome detail, even those customs, such as human
sacrifice in Thrace, which a Greek would surely find re-
pugnant at home (III 38); Plutarch disapprovingly calls
him a "Barbarian-lover,"[12] because he extends to these
northerners the moral exceptionalism of a latter-day anthropologist (IV 103). However the "Maneater" tribe of
yet more northern Scythia is just too savage even for him;
here he differs from certain contemporary students of
the Aztecs who find their institutional cannibalism un-
objectionable under the rubric of local custom and pro-
tein provision.[13] So too he holds his nose when reporting
Persian human sacrifice; I infer this from the fact that he
involves in this practice, apparently gratuitously, Xerxes'
wife, who is a repulsive creature (VII 114, IX 112).

The schema guiding the *History*, the conception of
Greek centrality, requires such respect, for where is the
glory in being contrasted to an insignificant or savage
Other? Herodotean opposition is not one of "positive/
negative," but of "this/other;" these Others are de-

12. "The Malice of Herodotus" 12.

13. The Aztecs had no large domesticated meat-providing
animals.

scribed as different rather than denigrated as primitives or nonentities. Their activities are taken seriously and their various splendors are appreciatively delineated—none of that dismissive colonial "the natives are restless tonight."

And yet, it is their very outlying topography that makes the Barbarians—how to put it?—the visited rather than the visitors, the studied rather than the students, the objects rather than the authors of history.[14] It is, furthermore, the very multifariousness of custom and language that turns the Persian force into a disparate, enslaved mass, whereas a Greek army marches as a consanguine, free (albeit squabbling) band. Herodotus, to be sure, delights in the description of the variety of nations that make up Xerxes' army (VII 61 ff.); of course he is emulating his poetic predecessor, who in the "Catalogue of Ships" of the *Iliad* (II 493 ff.) revels in a similar recital; furthermore, the very factuality of a roiled colorful variety, of a heavy barbaric splendor, with which he can trump Homer's fictitious roster, elicits comparison with the sober simplicity of the Greek hoplite, the nimble, lightly armed Marathon fighters (VI 112), and so contributes to the schematic antithesis of this "history."[15]

But it is time now to drop the notional scare quotes around the word history, and to sum up its meaning at

14. I remember only one report of a non-invasive Persian visitor to Greece, but I cannot find the place.

15. For all their gaudy panoply, the Persian archers were ill-equipped to meet the Greek spearmen, and, moreover, inferior in protective armor (IX 62).

this incipient, this Herodotean moment in its career. Unlike epic, history has a named author who writes prose. It is a second "showing-forth" following the primary display of human affairs, the result of an inquiry that gathers wonderful facts far and wide in the inhabited world, observes diverse customs with appreciative yet critical interest, traces events through time to far-off causes—and pinpoints the center of human affairs.

Thus the inquiry works in two dimensions, as we would say—aetiologically in time and schematically in space. This latter approach has as its presuppositions an unequal division of peoples into Greeks and Barbarians. The Barbarians are, as ethnic embodiments of a common humanity, objects of respectful interest, but they *are* peripheral, literally in surrounding geographically the land they unsuccessfully invade and figuratively in living without the chief human good—freedom.[16] Since Herodotus thinks the physical properties of a place, such as climate and productivity, are largely responsible for ethnic character, topography is causally revealing of a people's significance in the world; in other words, geography, conceived as a geometric schema accounts, in part, for the way nations figure in history (III 106, I 142). But again, a place and its customs have for Herodotus a hinterland of time and its events—which jibes with our general conception of history as essentially temporal. Yet, since it is the near-present world that is being explained, the temporal aetiology will be given by flash-

16. A strange fact: The detailed index in *The Landmark Herodotus* has many entries for "Slavery" but none for "Freedom"—the *crux* of the *History*.

backs, an old Homeric device. Flashbacks seem to me to require much mental sophistication, integrating the forward drive of a developing story with the grounding store of settled memory.

AFTER THE PRELUDE just explained, Herodotus launches immediately into the claims of the Persian "account-givers" or "prose-writers" (*logioi*, I 1) concerning the question: Who were the originating/responsible/blame-worthy/causal (*aitioi*) agents in the dispute between the Greeks and the Barbarians?[17] We know of no such Persian historians. We do not know whom Herodotus got to tell him this causal tale, according to which the Phoenicians began it all by carrying off, on a trading mission, some Greek women, among them Io; this was in dimmest mythical time, long before the abduction of Helen told of in the Homeric epics. I, for one, cannot tell whether Herodotus is speaking tongue-in-cheek in attributing this historization of Greek myth to the Persians and whether the invasive episodes that are supposed to give the remote causes of the Persian Wars are in fact a spoof of such aetiologies.[18] It is possible; Herodotus can be funny when debunking. Of a man said to have dived into the sea at Aphetai and to have come up nine miles away at Artemesium, he says dryly, "In my opinion he came by boat" (VIII 8). But

17. *Aitioi* has all four meanings.

18. In the comedy *The Acharnians*, Aristophanes parodies this woman-stealing litany, but perhaps it doesn't need a parody, being that already.

then, Herodotus is never in *dead* earnest, but ever *alive* with seriousness.

This beginning, however, raises three issues respectively in history, fiction, and philosophy, the first two already broached: Why don't the Persians have an inquiry called the *Hellenic Wars*? How are myths historically significant? The third is elicited by Herodotus's inquiry itself: What is the implied relation of history to philosophy?

First, then, those implausible Persian historians—why *are* all the accounts of the Persian War Greek? Was it because the invasion of Greece was a mere blip on the vast screen of the Persian empire and a mere ripple on the Great King's consciousness? Unlikely—Herodotus has learned that, under the pretext for a Greek offense, Xerxes intended that "we shall make the boundary of the land of Persia border on the realm of Zeus. The sun will not look down on any territory bordering our own . . ." (VII 8). The Greeks' check on his world conquest could not possibly be dismissed as a minor incident.

Was it perhaps that the very notion of a large-purposed inquiry was missing among the Persian scribes, or that a knowledgeable record of such a disaster would not have been welcome in Susa, or that a generous empathy with the Greeks was just not within the Persians' range of sensibility?—an empathy such as we find in Aeschylus's play *The Persians*,[19] set in Susa, in which the Queen Mother is shown mourning her son's defeat, and a pitiable Xerxes arrives back home—though, to be

---

19. Note that the Greek word for Persians, *Persai*, can be heard as "Sackers."

sure, a report of the Athenian spirit that won Salamis is not omitted. Or perhaps there was simply no venue for an audience suited to such a display: Cyrus, the founder of the Persian dynasty, had taunted the Greeks for having a space in the center of the city where they collect to cheat each other (I 153)—and it is in such a place, the *agora* (marketplace), that Herodotus would have performed his "showing-forth."

As for myth, the *History* begins with the above-mentioned deadpan account of the mythical cause of the Greek/Barbarian enmity—abductions of women. Of these pre-historical events, just before reality kicks in abruptly in c. 716 with a regime change in Lydia (I 7ff.), the main meeting ground of the two main antagonists, Herodotus says:

> That is what the Persians and Phoenicians say . . . I am not about to say that these things came about thus or otherwise. But I myself *do* know what man first began to commit unjust acts toward the Greeks.

That was Croesus, the Lydian King (I 5).

This admittedly unverifiable prehistory seems to me to serve three purposes: First, it raises and leaves unresolved the ultimate reason why Greeks and Barbarians are at odds, which is to say, there is no temporal aetiology, and thus no determinable assignment of blame—the causes are in their opposing natures. Recall here that the word "cause," *aitia*, carries with it a sense of accusation, of imputed blame, so that a blameless cause, a merely "formal" cause, such as a schema, is a very odd kind of cause, one first formulated in Aristotle's *Physics*

(II, 194b). Yet I think that some such causality is indeed implicit in Herodotean history: causation exercised by the configuration of nations.

Second, Herodotean prehistory raises the subject of the role of women—and puts it in its place. In the "Persian" accounts that Herodotus's pointed inquiry evidently elicited, the women cause events in public as victims, as stolen property. When the *History* enters real time, they recede into the bedroom where they are, however, highly causative; the first story giving the causes behind the institution of Croesus's dynasty turns on a woman's revenge for being shamed in her privacy (I 7). The power of women must have been on Herodotus's mind, for they seem to be both everything and nothing. He was born under a queen, Artemesia of Halicarnassus, who plays a ruthless, a manly, part in the sea battle of Salamis (VIII 87–88). Moreover, it is a mystifying fact I cannot imagine so astute an observer overlooking: the women of myth—Medea, Antigone, Clytemnestra—as portrayed in Attic drama are terrifyingly, publicly, potent. Where was that power in Herodotus's Athens? His account does somewhat qualify the tragedians' depiction of dramatic women, bringing it down to earth; he seems almost to countermand the tragedians compensatory elevation of women into terrific causal forces. It is a Herodotean mode, this damping skepticism, quite compatible with, in fact—as I think—the enabling complement of, his reverent delight in wondrous grandeur.

The third purpose of what might be called the "mythology" of the *History*, its purposeful use of myths, is for the sanguine nullification of Homeric epic in favor of Herodotean inquiry. He spends eight paragraphs (II 112–120) providing testimony that Helen was never in Troy but spent those ten years of the Greek invest-ment of Ilium in Egypt. As I mentioned, the Egyptian priests he consulted said that Helen's husband, Menel-aus, himself was the source of this revisionism (II 108).[20] Thus Homer's *Iliad* is really about nothing, its poetic point supplanted by the findings of Herodotus's *History*. For here he says cunningly that he believed the priests, because it made sense that, if Helen had been in Troy, the Trojans, reasonable Barbarians, would have given her back (II 120). Thus the first great invasion, which went from West to East, was a futile overreaction on the part of the Greeks—the blame game shifts to the other side with the beginning of real history. When the tide of invasion turns around, from Asia to Greece, the remote causes offer, as I said, no viable moral hold.

Let me here sum up what I discern about the impor-tance of Homer's epics in and for Herodotus's *History*. To my mind, the first great Greek writer of prose was in a—partly implicit—contest with the first great Greek writer of verse,[21] both in deriding and in rivaling him.

---

20. The story was told earlier by the poet Stesichorus (born c. 630) in his lost *Palinode*, and later by Euripides in his play *Helen* (412).

21. Not least with respect to size: Homer's 27,000-plus lines against Herodotus's 1,500-plus paragraphs; Herodotus trumps Homer perhaps by one-fifth. It is not known whether Homer actu-ally dictated his epics (like Milton) or they were codified and writ-ten down later. If so, probably in Athens, perhaps by the tyrant Peisistratus in the sixth century (Cicero, *On the Orator* III 137).

He accomplishes the former, as I have reported, by cutting the object of the Trojan War out of the *Iliad* (II 112 ff.), by discrediting Homer's geography (II 23), and by reducing him in age to Hesiod's contemporary and in rank to his equal (II 53). He emulates Homer by providing a magnificent inventory of Xerxes' army to compare with Homer's "Catalogue of Ships" (VII 61 ff.; *Iliad* II 484 ff.). And—I will dwell on this below—he establishes a hero to rival both Odysseus the level-headed advisor of the *Iliad*, and Odysseus the cunning poet-liar of the *Odyssey*.

Yet one more point in this rivalry with Homer, in which Herodotus would seem to have a hard row to hoe, though he goes about it cleverly: Aristotle famously says that the difference between a historian and a poet is not meter or no meter, and that, if Herodotus's work (he names him) were put in meter it would still be history. "But they differ in this, that the former tells what *has* come to be and the latter what *might* come to be. Therefore poetry is more philosophical and more serious than history. For poetry tells more of universal things (*ta katholou*), history of each particular" (*Poetics* 1451b).

This passage echoes Herodotus's prelude, in which he says that he will show forth "what has come to be." He has subverted—before the fact, of course—Aristotle's implicit subordination of his history to Homer's poetry, by treating the epics as *factually falsifiable*, as inferior history: Homer deliberately chose the false Helen story as more "well-fitting" to epic (II 116)—to the discredit of poetry, Herodotus implies. To borrow a phrase from a poet who is herself critical of poetry: Homer has con-

cocted "real cities with imaginary princesses."[22] It makes
the poet, from the point of view of telling how things are
in fact, neither fish nor fowl—real venues (at least in the
Iliad), real people (Helen), false circumstances. History
is, Herodotus implies, purer. Its tall tales are reported
as "historically" indisputable, as the accurate product of
his inquiry: people do in fact believe and report them,
and so they are legitimately recorded history.

Now, brought to the brink of historical factuality in
the *History*, and having set out some of the elements of
Herodotus's self-definition in opposition to Homer, the
moment has come to distinguish his inquiry from philosophy, which Aristotle cites as poetry's superior rival,
and which Herodotus leaves out as beyond his brief.

Herodotus, it seems to me, is one of those individuals
who exemplify, concentratedly and pungently, Greek-
ness. Like his fictional voyaging predecessor, he "wan-
dered much . . . and saw the towns of human beings and
knew their mind" (*Odyssey* I 1–3). But unlike Odysseus,
his mind is not on collecting loot, ladies, and adventures,
but on comprehending the inhabited world's variety in
a schema through deliberate, open-eyed inquiry (*historia*). Now the Greeks, or rather some of them, engage
in another typical activity: the non-sensual search (*zetesis*) for a single but invisible realm behind the appear-
ing world. In other words, the Greeks *and they alone*
know spatiotemporal inquiry *and* non-sensual search—

---

22. Marianne Moore, "Poetry," a poem whose first line is "I,
too, dislike it," and which goes on to speak of poetry as presenting
"'imaginary gardens with real toads in them.'"

history and philosophy. Only they, both driven by wonder, know each and both.

The difference between the two pursuits is not one between empirical fact-gathering followed by inductive conceptualization, as opposed to rational laying down of axioms preceding deductive propositions, since both of these activities begin with keen observation guided by some basic presuppositions. The difference, as it touches an understanding of Herodotus, is in the explanatory outcome: not primarily a *theory* discovered by *introspection*, by thoughtful going-within, but what I have called a *schema*, a quasi-spatial world diagram discovered by *circumspection*, so to speak, thoughtful looking-about in the world, by going out to gather in its regions, lands, cities, customs.

I cannot imagine that Herodotus did not think something like this out, indeed had it preliminarily in mind as he planned his travels, and that he did not distinguish his way only from that of the epic poets, Homer above all, but also from the so-called "physicists" of his own native Ionia. These were the first inquirers into the material and motions of what we call nature, though among them he mentions only Thales, who was also an engineer and politician (I 70 ff.). These "physicists" might be called "protophilosophers." Their successors are the philosophers, who search for the immaterial beings and powers at the roots of the cosmos, a third group, of whom he says nothing.[23] The first of them, Heraclitus,

23. Herodotus uses a philosophy-word, *philosopheon*, just once (I 30), in a context where it means "wanting wisdom," the

who died just about when Herodotus was born (c. 480), was his neighbor in Ionian Ephesus. Indeed, philosophy arose at the margins: the other founder was Parmenides in Italian Elea; they are describable as engaged in one enterprise though in antithetical ways. Herodotus, moreover, stayed in Athens, evidently while composing and reciting the *History*.[24] While in Athens, how could he have failed to meet Socrates, with whom philosophy, "the affect of wonder" (*Theaetetus* 155d), had moved to the center, and who was only a decade or so younger (b. 470) than he himself? He may have compared their ways and so defined, by distinguishing them, his own. He would control the massive material subject to his inquiry by zeroing in not on human essence but on ethnic type. And this inquiry was not contemplative search but observational research.

My point is this: I think it is plausible to conjecture that his way, his *inquiry*, was deliberately developed; his "showing-forth" seems to me to be loaded with purpose and intention. He had, I think, clearly developed techniques for going about inquiring: he was evidently introduced to the best informants—priests, court officials, knowledgeable dignitaries, storytellers, and retailers of

---

kind gotten by traveling all over the earth for the sake of "observation" (*theoria*). The prephilosophical usage of two terms central to the inquiry into supersensual being, which came to be called philosophy, could be taken as a sign that Herodotus is distancing himself from that activity. Of course, it's just a conjecture.

24. He died in Italian Thurii, an Athenian colony he had joined, c. 425.

hearsay (II 29). He gained access to records, temple ar-
chives, and monuments. Moreover, like a good inter-
viewer, he came prepared with questions, which were,
in fact, so neatly directed that, it seems to me, they often
skewed the answers of obliging respondents. Sometimes
he followed up and verified information by traveling to
a different venue, say from Memphis to Thebes to see if
priestly tales jibed (II 2–3), or to see a reputed wonder
such as the plumed serpents of Arabia (II 75).

His pride is thus his *autopsia*, "seeing-for-oneself"
(II 29, 99; III 115), a Greek word, which like many,
has deteriorated in adoption, from beholding wonders
to inspecting corpses.[25] One might say that Herodotus's keen sight-seeing is just the technique that blind
Homer couldn't and sighted philosophers needn't have
employed—it's yet another way of distinguishing the
wonders preserved by history from the wonders visual-
ized in poetry—and both from the wonder that moves
philosophy.

Of course, Herodotus's enterprise required travel—
and what a hazardous, often tedious, always uncomfortable journeying it must have been! Though of all this
he says nothing: sailing with capricious winds and in la-
boriously oar-driven, slow merchantmen; slow trekking
with slow, hot, sand-scoured caravans; anxiously con-
veying fragile papyri filled with invaluable notes. I imag-

25. The meaning of *autopsia* is related to *historia* in this way:
a *histor* is an eyewitness; the word is related to a form of the verb
"to know" (*ismen*; "we know"), which is in turn related to a form
of the verb "to see" (*eidenai*). *Histor*, however, doesn't occur in
the *History*.

ine that he secured his place at the table and rewarded the hospitality extended to him with storytelling—as had his unreal predecessor in voyaging, Odysseus.

Though one may well *imagine* that Homeric Odysseus's loot-gathering piracy was in fact only a pretext for sight-and-wonder-seeing, Herodotus was the first Greek we *know* of who traveled just to see for himself.[26] The Phoenician sailors were usually commercial travelers; Greeks were often colonizers—Naucratis in Egypt is an early example (II 178).

In the "mythology" considered above, we saw Herodotus introducing himself as a critically disposed reader of reports. In the "history" proper, we see him as an eyewitness self-trained in estimating credibility; he expresses judgments concerning what he hears—*autopsia* of course includes *akoe*, "hearsay," or better "aural reports," (II 29)—in degrees: acceptance, preference, rejection, abstention from opinion, decision of undecidability, (e.g., I 5, IV 11, II 88). He forms his judgments on the basis of various criteria: common sense, general rationality, particular inference (VI 121, II 33). His basic principle is, "What is told me by each [informant], that I write down as heard" (II 123), which is not incompatible with discretion; he does not tell all (*ibid.*). This is

---

26. There were, besides a shadowy predecessor, Hecataeus, also commissioned exploratory sailors (IV 43, *Landmark Herodotus* V 125, note). Solon "made a pretense" of "sight-seeing" (*theoria*, "spectacle-viewing," "observation;" later, in philosophy, "contemplation," as in Note 23); he had given the Athenians a constitution that put them on the way to democracy, and he left so as to escape being forced to alter it (I 29).

the rule that goes with his wide view of history: It concerns not only what is the case, but also, or even more, as I said, what people believe; a desiccated "nothing but the facts" report would be less humanly adequate. One might say that Herodotus does an end run around arid factuality. Recall that most of Herodotus's history deals with the front end of the past, the near present that is still vivid to some of the living. Moreover, he is reporting on peoples whose time-sense is such that the past is not passed and bygone but present and now at work.

Latter-day, academic history all but defines itself as concerned with the past that is gone, that is, with a temporal excerpt of past time, often irrecoverably disconnected from the present by the impossibility of being eyewitnessed or even documented; indeed to become adept in historical research is to learn to make much of little, though that life-deprived little may grow large in expository bulk. Such past-history therefore labors under a double liability: first, the vanishing of a plenitude of vital evidence, the kind that is lost when contemporaries die, and the second, the difficulty of establishing a real—not just analogous—connection to the present so as to escape the charge of irrelevance to the current situation.[27] Herodotus, however, is writing from c. 450 to

27. An acute meditation on temporal disruption occurs in Kierkegaard's *Philosophical Fragments* (1844), Ch. V, "The Disciple at Second Hand." There the issue is that "1843 years have elapsed between the contemporary disciple" of Christ and the present. If Christ is a fact of history "contemporaneity is a *desideratum*." How then is faith, which is a belief in *existence*, in *fact*, possible for the latter-day disciple?

420, roughly within two generations of the three great battles of Xerxes' expedition. So multiple tales—causal, explanatory, illustrative—abound, and he welcomes these as the things "that have come to be by the agency of human beings." He is not bound by demanding protocols of established historical research that may screen out (if time has not already done it) what matters, namely, the aetiological, hence motivating myths that people then *believed*. Moreover he is not hampered by notions of efficient causality or chains of causation, so time-breaks, for which research comes up empty and the continuity of events is disrupted, don't impinge on his account. His history offers, besides enchanting curiosities, an ever-pertinent ethnographic design, persuasively documented.

I want to return for a moment to the role of these probably non-factual tales, to show how they seem to me to gain their legitimacy. This story is a favorite for inclusion in "Tales from Herodotus" because it is funny; schoolchildren used to know it. It even made it into *The Great Gatsby*.

Kleisthenes, tyrant of Sicyon in the Peloponnesus, wanted to find the best husband for his daughter Agariste. So he invited all who thought themselves worthy to come to his city for a year to be vetted. Here's Herodotus:

> From Italy came Smindyrides of Sybaris . . . From Athens came Megacles, son of Alcmaeon and . . . Hippocleides . . . who was prominent among the Athenians in both wealth and good looks . . . Those were all the suitors that came . . . (VI 127 ff.)

—and they stayed the year.

Here's Fitzgerald:

> I wrote down . . . the names of those who came to
> Gatsby's house that summer . . . From East Egg,
> then, came the Chester Beckers . . . From West Egg
> came the Poles and the Mulreadys . . . and Newton
> Orchid, who controlled Films Par Excellence . . .

And so the whole catalogue of all who took advantage
of Gatsby's lavish hospitality, until, finally, there is this
nimble, mostly trochaic line (⁻˘): "All these people came
to Gatsby's house in the summer"—and some stayed on
(*The Great Gatsby*, ch. 4).

Now Kleisthenes himself preferred Hippocleides. But
came the parting feast at the year's end, and this dec-
orous engagement party turned, as did Gatsby's party,
into a drunken rout. Hippocleides climbed on a table,
danced in various styles, and then stood on his head
waving his legs. Kleisthenes, disgusted, told him that he
had just danced away his bride, to which he famously
replied, "No worries to Hippocleides." So the other
Athenian, Megacles, got Agariste. The end.

But there are pointers both to past and future. Looking
backwards: Megacles' father, Alcmaeon, had, Herodotus
says, won his great wealth by taking tricky advantage of
Croesus, king of Lydia, the first fully historical Asian to
be in touch with mainland Greeks (VI 125). The Alcmaeonids, so empowered, became famous as tyrant-haters
(VI 121, 123). Croesus also played host to another Athenian, Solon, who had framed the earliest plan for Athenian democracy (I 29). Since both Alcmaeon and Solon
probably lived at least a generation before Croesus, the

Lydian venue for these remote progenitors of Athenian democracy is not factual, but it helps to establish Greek cosmopolitanism in general and Athenian complexity—canny dealing and love of freedom—in particular.

Looking forwards: Alcmaeon's son Megacles in turn had a son by Agariste, a second Kleisthenes, who established an actual democracy in Athens (VI 131). Megacles' granddaughter, another Agariste, dreamed that she gave birth to a lion and bore Pericles—Pericles the Alcmaeonid, *the* great man of *The Peloponnesian War*. He is named only once in *The Persian Wars* (VI 131). But his name is an ominous reminder, *in media res*, that the glorious Persian Wars had a calamitous aftermath, the first decade of which Herodotus lived through.

The Hippocleides anecdote and the Croesus story thus throw a raking light on the family fortune and the family name of the great man of the first glorious, then fatal post-Persian decades. Pericles was known for his reticent gravity (Plutarch, *Pericles* 5), but his fortune was the gold gained by the great-great-grandfather's, crafty greed; his descent through a marriage achieved by the good fortune of a too nonchalant rival suitor disqualified. Is Herodotus implying, though he labors to defend the Alcmaeonids (VI 121 ff.), that it is better to be a "new man"—Themistocles, who will be shown to be his hero?

Herodotus makes few and veiled references to the next, the disastrous Peloponnesian War. The most direct is his comment on the Delian earthquake of 490. He does not mention that the island became the venue of the Delian League, the vehicle of Athens' hegemony;

it had been formed by the Greek cities for the continuing defense of Greece against the Persians. The Athenians, who had been entrusted with its leadership, seized the League's treasury at Delos, into which members were paying dues. They used this loot in building the Parthenon (447–432); Herodotus was there to see it and—like myself—may have wondered whether publicly to deplore but privately to applaud the misappropriation. But he does interpret the event from hindsight: He supposes it was the gods' portent, revealing to men the evils to come, worse ones than had ever befallen the Greeks before. Some were caused by the Persians, but others by the chief Greek powers "making war about dominion" (*arche*, VI 98, that is, empire). And of course, Pericles was, one might argue, the instigator of that civil war; it is the view expressed in *Federalist* No. 63. But Herodotus suppresses all that and only implies that the gods themselves had marked the place, the future site of the league's treasury, whence were to issue the post-Persian evils.

Both the beginning and the end of the *History* might be taken, not implausibly, to make oblique reference to Athens' downfall. Early on, Herodotus says that cities that were anciently great are now mostly small, and the reverse; knowing that human fortune never stays fixed, he will take note of both equally (I 5). Of course, Athens is great in Herodotus's present, but I can imagine him imagining, when he left for Italy, what she would soon descend to.

Finally, the very last paragraph of the *History* recurs to Cyrus, the founder of the invading dynasty, to tell a story of conquest foregone (IX 121). Cyrus is a born king, kingly by nature (I 114 ff., in Greek *Kyros* means "Lord").[28] This wisely royal Cyrus was approached by some Persians with a proposal to leave their small and harsh country and to appropriate a better land from those over whom they ruled. Cyrus told them to go ahead and find a new location, but to prepare no longer to be rulers but ruled: "from soft sites, soft men come to be."[29] Now there is some question whether the *History* is complete. It seems to me this disconcerting ending may well encapsulate Herodotus's final fear for Athens—and, incidentally, prove the book to be finished—though soft living was not, in the end, their chief failing. Their volatility and the luxurious indiscipline of their young leader Alcibiades were indeed their danger (Thucydides VI, 15), together with their unwillingness to be content with what they had (VI 9).

IT IS TIME TO set out how Herodotus captures this glorious and endangered center of the world, Athens. First, here are some pertinent lines from Constantine Cavafy's

28. And is thus represented by Xenophon in his *Cyropaedia*, "Education of Cyrus" (early 4th cent.). This book employs a mode the reverse of the one I am attributing to Herodotus: It turns Barbarian otherness into Hellenicity, using Greek lineaments to portray a Persian as a model of the good monarch.

29. Oddly, early on in the *History* (I 126), Cyrus takes the opposite tack. He persuades the Persians to revolt from the Medes by the prospect of luxury. Was Herodotus nodding or was Cyrus double-tongued?

poem "Waiting for the Barbarians." The city is assembled, waiting for the invaders. Then:

> Why this sudden restlessness, this confusion?
> (How serious people's faces have become.)
> Why are the streets and squares emptying so rapidly,
> everyone going home so lost in thought?

>> Because night has fallen and the barbarians have
>>   not come.
>> And some who have just returned from the
>>   border say
>> there are no barbarians any longer.

> And now, what's going to happen to us without
>   barbarians?
> They were, those people, a kind of solution.

Failing to be overrun by barbarians is confounding because their invasion concentrates the civilized mind. The Persians will do some such thing for the Hellenes—as their historian saw it: In coming, they defined them; in leaving, they disconcerted them.

My idea is, then, that Herodotus defines, now explicitly, now implicitly, the Greek-speaking nation, Hellas, by its *oppositions*: its common Hellenic characteristics, realized in antithetical yet typically Greek city-states, its conduct of a common war of survival led by men of opposite yet typically Greek temperaments—this whole, internally contrasting complex having been encompassed, delimited, and defined by the basic opposition of Barbarian and Greek.

These Barbarians encircle the Greeks both notionally and literally. Herodotus underwrites his ethnographic description by a geographic layout, a sort of topographic Euler diagram[30] (to speak anachronistically) in which Greece lies at the center and the barbarian nations and tribes circumscribe it at expanding distances. In this figure, Herodotus might be said, as in my title, to "comprehend" the Greeks by non-Greeks, a central human phenomenon by a variety of outliers—all within the circle of universal humanity. But the circle *has* a center. Thus Herodotus is at once a descriptive ethnographer, that is, a student of human beings in their nationally specified humanity, and an evaluative anthropologist, in the sense of tracing human distinction in both senses: difference and excellence. All, the monolingual Greeks and polyglot Barbarians, have produced "great and wonderful works," yet Greeks are differently different.

Herodotus's world, the inhabited earth, is, as I've reported, not neatly encircled by a perfectly round *okeanos*; he laughs at current travel descriptions (*periodoi*) giving a perfectly symmetrical view of earth (IV 36). Homer lets the north shade into the murky domain of the dead across the world-bounding ocean (xi 13). For Herodotus it is an unexplored expanse; the kind marked on early European maps by HERE BE DRAGONS. The same holds for the other quarters: the territories at the extremes exceed by far the explored, inhabited earth, the human world.

---

30. A logician's diagram representing class inclusion, participation, or exclusion by circles that might be included, intersecting, or external.

Herodotus's *Inquiry* proceeds around the inhabited interior whose own interior is the Mediterranean, the "Midland" sea, into which juts the Greek mainland. Thus:

Book I. To the East. The Lydians are the interface between Greeks and their main and most defining opponents, *the* Barbarians of the *History*, the Persians.

Book II. To the South. The Egyptians, the upsidedown people in an inverted land, represent, by a sort of anti-symmetry, the most literal defining antitheses to the Greeks.

Book IV. To the Northeast and North. The Scythians, by their semi-savagery, define and literally delimit Greek civilization.

Scattered through the *History*: To the West is the future-fraught region—Italy, the venue for the emigration of Greeks under pressure, the first of these being the fleeing Trojans under Aeneas, the founder of Rome, and the most recent Herodotus, colonist of Athenian Thurii. Yet farther west, is the Atlantic Ocean beyond the Pillars of Heracles (Straits of Gibraltar).

The West will not figure much in my encirclement story. The Hellenic Phocaeans have colonized Iberia (Spain, I 163), but those who sail past the Pillars turn south toward Africa (IV 12, 195). The Atlantic itself will wait something short of two millennia to be crossed, long after northwestern Europe has opened up. America, the new-found-land of modernity, Bacon's Atlantis,[31]

---

31. Francis Bacon, *New Atlantis* (1627). That this Christianized research facility, benevolent and ominous, could be interpreted as our America is my imaginative construction.

will be "discovered" by Europeans, as once the Barbarians were explored by the Greeks—the ever-repeated and ever-burdened relation of those who are discovered and those who uncover them.[32] We too, the alpha-Barbarians of the West, were thus explored—what a great moment in ethnography it would be to hear our Herodotus, Tocqueville, in conversation with his Greek forebear!

FOR ALL THE REGIONS, peoples, events of his world, Herodotus has organizing schemata. For climate, the extremes of the "inhabited [world]" (*oikoumene*) have been assigned the finest products, but the Greeks have been assigned the most finely temperate seasons (III 106)—Asian Ionia, Herodotus's region, above all (I 142). For mobility, the Persians expand, the Egyptians are fixed, the Scythians roam, the Greeks travel. Plato will specify this schema by character: Thracians, Scythians, and the people "up there" have spirit, the people "by us" love learning, and the Phoenicians and Egyptians crave money (*Republic* 436e ff.). In the *History*, too, more specific layouts will continue to turn up. So now to these surrounding Barbarians themselves.

The Persians. The Persians are not only the non-Greek principals of the *History*, but as eventual possessors of a huge empire, whose complete world-domination the small Greek nation prevents, they are the ligature binding all the Barbarians together: Cyrus conquers Lydia,

---

32. Which is now coming to an end as the supply of first-contact people runs out, and the ever-studied are rebelling against these inherently intrusive anthropological attentions.

Cambysis Egypt, Darius Scythia. Consequently they are themselves comparative ethnographers of a sort[33] and explorers, though not for the sake of sight-seeing (IV 43); for example, Darius sent an expedition down the Indus for strategic reasons, to subjugate the Indians (IV 44).

But it is near the coast of Asia Minor that the Greeks first meet Persians, and Persians come to hear of the Greeks. The Lydian king Croesus tells his Persian conqueror, Cyrus, of Athens' "wise man" (*sophistes*, I 29) Solon, the author of a constitution that prefigures her democracy (I 86); this same Croesus is the first to have a later often repeated experience with the Spartan allies: they arrive too late (I 70) and are generally reluctant to move (I 152). The Lydians have some affinity to the Greeks. They are inventive—coinage, retailing, games— and not sessile. And, of course, the Persians are in direct contact with the Ionians of the coastal cities whom they try, a rebellious and critical lot, to incorporate into their expanding empire and among whom were born

33. King Darius interrogates Greeks at his court about their burial customs. (*N.B.* Once again, we rarely hear of Persians visiting prominent Greeks.) For how much money, he asks, would they eat the corpses of their fathers?—for no amount. Later he summons some Indians, who do just that, and asks them for what reward they would burn their dead; they are offended at the very thought. Herodotus concludes that the poet Pindar is right, "Custom is King" (III 38). I repeat this story because Herodotus, if queried, might have modified himself: Custom (*nomos*) is King in the realm of custom, but how much of human action is custom-driven is just the Herodotean question. Pindar was a Greek, and once you articulate what Custom does, his throne and rule is shaken. Above all, the Athenians, or at least their model types, are infraction-prone.

Homer (probably), Thales, Heraclitus (not mentioned by Herodotus), and Herodotus himself.

In accordance with Herodotus's way of interweaving history (in our sense of chronological eventuation) and ethnography, the pre-war account of the rising Persian empire is spread through Books I–V. The stories of the war-kings, Darius and Xerxes, is told in Books VII–IX. I shall wait to set out Xerxes' personal counterparts among the Greeks until I have delineated the contrasting nations of the early books; in the later books these will, as it were, be taking on individual human shape.

Here then is a selective summary of the Persian ethnography (I 131–140). Persians worship nature. They have no statues or altars but sacrifice to natural features and elements, such as sun and rivers, earth and fire. Their chief god is the sky, which Herodotus calls Zeus (evidently Ahura Mazda); so they need no temples or statues and have few sacrificial rituals (I 131–132). Equals kiss each other on the mouth, inferiors prostrate themselves. They honor most those who live closest to them and less those who live further away. They adopt foreign customs, but only a few from the Greeks, for instance, pederasty.

Their male children learn to ride, shoot the bow, and speak the truth. Lying is a man's most shameful act. They are forbidden even to speak of what it is forbidden to do.

What would a Greek, an Athenian, think? My conjecture: "Our gods have human shape, and although they disguise themselves in familiar mortals' form, 'they are plainly known,' if only by their tracks (*Iliad* XIII 72). We make pictures and statues of these gods, and we know well that these are human artifacts; we often know who painted or carved them, for example, Exekias and Phidias. We even figure for ourselves strange, complex juxtapositions. In his *Eumenides*, our poet Aeschylus brings onstage an Athena who confronts a statue of herself; it induces in some of us complex thoughts about original and image—complex, since the stage-Athena is herself mimetic. Our city is, after all, called *Athenai*, 'the Athenas,' Athen*s*—the city of multiple Athenas; we are used to having her before us in multiples, as so many sacred items, indeed we rejoice in our many gods' multiple images. But though we have never seen the goddess herself, we know that if she did not have an—albeit invisible— form, every presentation of her would be (in principle) a misrepresentation, and if she did not have human form, and we, conversely, divine lineaments, every attempt of mutual understanding (except for incantations and omens) would be futile. So we do not so much *believe in* her (a phrase we do not use) as experience and acknowledge her. Your nature-bound divinities are enormous but surd, opaque powers; our immortal mortals in their limited shapelines are responsive, limpid gods."

So might a Greek, reading Herodotus, think, so might he himself have thought, articulating his own tradition in contrast to Persian religion. So also would a Greek wonder what kind of upbringing would leave a boy without any civilizing relation to the Muses, what human being would consent to prostrate himself, and why honor should be proportional to distance rather than excellence. But above all, I imagine Greeks balking at the injunction against articulating what it is bad to do and at the absolute prohibition against lying. The former would do away with tragedy, poetry being the special venue for speaking fascinatingly about evil, and among the Greeks this aspect, especially of tragedy, induces a deep discussion concerning the attractive imaging of badness (Plato, *Republic* 377 ff.). The latter, the Persian national prohibition against false speech, would have undone the hero of the *History*—Themistocles. Of that, more below—and of what these simple, archaic customs of the Persians eventually produced.

The Egyptians. Herodotus now moves south to Egypt, which was brought into the compass of the *History* by incorporation into the Persian empire. He extends his account of Egypt to sixty-three paragraphs (II 35–98) because of the plenitude of its wonders, and because it is so "different," so "other in kind" (*heteroion, alloion,* II 35). Egypt is indeed a wonderful land, though somewhat less in the sense of admiration than of amazement. It is the *inverse* land, the upside-down land. That implies, of course, that Greece is the right-side-up land, a take now termed "ethnocentric."[34] I don't think Herodotus revels in invidious distinctions. Nonetheless,

34. Of course my whole point is that the *History* is a most deliberately ethnocentric work. The question would then be, whether is it unwarrantedly so, but that is the very question the latter-day epithet means to forestall: Does the human world have a "privileged" center whence flows a heritage beyond time and place? Never, on ethnographic principle? Now and then, until "things fall apart"? Always, by the continual relocation of a world spirit? Herodotus occupies the middle position, I think.

his motive, right behind the showing forth of great and wonderful things, is, I've claimed, to define the Greeks in distinction from the Barbarians; the latter, though appreciated for themselves in their own *part* of the *History*, serve to center the Greeks through the *whole*.

First then, the Egyptian geography is, to Herodotus's topographical vision, upside down. The river, whose alluvial deposits are the constituting gift to the country (II 5, 17), flows north, toward the central sea. In fact, Herodotus does not speak of "flowing north" or "traveling south," but of going "upstream" on the Nile.[35] He does not view the Earth from a cosmic perspective, as will the astronomers of the European hemisphere, who see it as a celestial body, with a pole pointing north at the North Star, Polaris, and its invisible southern tip below, pointed at the Southern Cross (neither name is ancient); he surveys it rather as a terrestrial expanse, from whose opposite unexplored extremes he moves inward. The sources of the Nile are in this unknown territory (II 34).

Not only the flooding, land-making, seasonal river is strange, but also the climate (he says "sky"). There are no seasons. Even more to be wondered at are the customs. The women go to the marketplace to sell, while the men stay at home and weave. Sophocles picked this up in *Oedipus at Colonus*, whose Oedipus derides his unhelpful sons for having taken on the customs of Egypt, where males stay at home weaving while their

---

35. In fact, though the Nile does flow north in its lower reaches, its counterpart, the Danube, was known by him to flow largely west-east.

wives provide a livelihood (337 ff.). But that is not the tone of Herodotus's report; he simply wonders and tells.

There is much more detail concerning inverted gender differences: for example, men carry loads on their heads, women on their shoulders. Men pee sitting down, women standing up. And the Egyptians alone practice circumcision.[36]

They are exceedingly pious. Their priesthood is ritual-ridden, especially concerning sacrifices. Some of their gods are beast-headed, as is only Pan among the Greeks.[37] The few wild animals found in Egypt are all sacred; domestic cats too are cherished and embalmed (II 66–67). Herodotus reports at length their methods of embalming humans (II 86–90). Their oracles are never human, only divine, and their priests are never women, only men (II 83, 35).

In sum, all of the Egyptians who live on arable land are by far the most "learned of chroniclers" (*logiotatoi*) who "foster memory" more than any others of whom Herodotus has experience; so, "following paternal customs they acquire none in addition" (II 77, 79).

36. The monotheistic circumcising Hebrews were below Herodotus's radar. (I have omitted Herodotus's history of that transit-region, the Levant, and of African Libya [III, IV passim], which do, however, fit into the schema.) There are other, stranger, omissions, above all of Akhnaton, the proto-monotheistic pharaoh (d. 1362), who briefly introduced sun worship, and whose memory the priestly establishment had probably suppressed.

37. Pan, with goats' ears, horns, and hoofs, is a strange, vague, isolated, haunting god—above all the gods if his name is construed to mean "All," but below them for his animal form and passions. The Greeks do, in fact, have some of everything.

The above reports a tiny part of the details concerning sacred practices, which Herodotus has collected from a people that is "excessively scrupulous in religious observances." He knows much more than he tells; he especially avoids speaking of "divine matters" and only mentions them when "overtaken by necessity" (II 65). What necessity? I imagine it might be the contribution a sacred practice might make to the inverted-land depiction. Why the reluctance? I imagine that it is partly tact, respect for information given him as a presumably discreet visitor, partly a sense that anthropological detail, while always interesting, is not always significant—or, more accurately, that it sometimes obscures the universality of "divine matters" by excessively localizing them, by emphasizing "local divinity" (*epichorios theos*, V 102, IX 119).

This Egypt, then, holds, as it were, a mirror up to Greece in which it beholds itself inverted. (Recall that mirror images are lateral inverses: My proper right eye is my image's proper left.) But Egypt is not only inverted in space; it is also flipped qualitatively, anti-symmetrically. Not the least of it is that Egypt is river-made, alluvial, and climateless, while Greece is sea-girt, rocky, and seasonal. Egypt, moreover, is the land where the dead, embalmed and encased, remain, semi-immortal mortals, among the living, housed in luxurious tombs. (Not quite logically, though very humanly, the Egyptians carry around a realistically painted wooden corpse at their dinners as a reminder to the yet living to enjoy themselves before they are like that statue, II 78.) As the Persians let bodies be picked clean by birds before entombment, some Indians eat corpses (I 140, III 38), and the Egyptians maintain them marinated, so the Greeks wash and then bury or burn their dead, letting dust go to dust, in earth or by fire.

Thus, for all the art their anthropomorphic gods elicit, the Greeks are more natural by far than the Egyptians and indeed than most Barbarians, since it takes worldliness for humans to become natural; hide-bound tribalism tends to be artifice-ridden. The alien veneration of animals, and, by contrast, the very existence of their own beautiful anthropomorphic gods must bring home to Greeks their proper integration into a natural cosmos, a well-ordered world in which humans do not worship lower species, but live in a continuity of appearance and in a great chain of being with the higher orders. Similarly are their women properly integrated into the world. Although they do, to be sure, stay mostly at home, they are, on the other hand, revered as high priestesses; the Athenians are named after their goddess, who is served by a priestess (VIII 41). Moreover, the Delphic Pythia is a central power in Greece, and the chief temple of the Hellenes, Apollo's shrine, is her seat at Delphi, whence she speaks to the Greeks, saying what they need to hear: "Nothing too much;" the Egyptians say to themselves, evidently requiring encouragement: "Drink and enjoy." So, the Egyptians, who are *rigor mortis* incarnate, past-devoted, show the Greeks by antithesis what it is to be alive. Greek records of the past are none too meticulous and full of vividly inventive emendation, while their female-framed oracles are witty, elusive, and quite influence-prone. And though not impious, Greeks can take their gods lightly, and with delight. Read in the *Odyssey*, for example, about the locked-in congress of Ares and Aphrodite, quite literally caught in adultery by the net of her lame husband, Hephaestus (viii 266 ff.).

In sum, the Greeks must feel themselves to be young in the face of the Egyptians. In fact, not in the *History* but in a Platonic dialogue, an old Egyptian priest says to Solon, who was visiting Egypt ". . . you Greeks are ever children . . . young in soul."[38] The word "young" is *neoi*; it means both "young" and "new." He goes on to say that none of their opinions are derived from "ancient hearsay" (*Timaeus* 22 a–c, *History* I 30), which implies that the Greeks are not tradition-bound, but are receptive to new notions; for them alone, as I intimated, custom is *not* king—or perhaps rather an elected king, subject to recall.

This is the moment to say something about Greek receptivity. Herodotus comes to regard it, as he makes his circuit through the Barbarians, not as flat imitation but as transforming absorption. He thinks—a remarkable idea—that Greek rituals were borrowed from the older Egyptian practices and that, in fact, the Greek pantheon was adopted wholesale from the Egyptian (II 53, 58). Old wine in new bottles. What was desiccated and rigidified in Egyptian Thebes and Memphis was rejuvenated

38. Solon, as I said, was the first historical sightseer traveling for the sake of observation (*theoria*), as had fictional Odysseus before him. I should remind the reader that the note-taker Herodotus himself had a forerunner in Hecataeus (late sixth century), author of a lost *Voyage Around the World*; Herodotus used and criticized it.

by Homer and Hesiod in Asian Ionia and mainland Boeotia: ancient chronicles brought to life in poetry, stiff statues revivified (after a period of acculturation called "archaic" by us) as supple gods—off went the starchy hieratic costumes; deities and humans were both re-dressed or undressed, the female in diaphanous robes, the males *au naturel*. But, of course, the old wine turned young in the transfusion—tart and fresh.

Solon brought home to Athens from Egypt a political law requiring transparency, which Herodotus praises. Once a year, everyone must declare how he makes his living (II 177). While the Greeks got their first astro-nomical instrument from the Babylonians,[39] Herodotus thinks they got geometry, here still in its literal meaning, "earth-measurement," from its Egyptian discoverers.

So by and large the Greeks gather good ideas wher-ever they find them, while the Barbarians in general are not so reciprocally receptive to Greek ways.[40] The Egyp-tians don't change, evidently impervious to novelty, "nor

---

39. It was a sundial, consisting of a pointer (*gnomon*, "knower"), mounted on a hemisphere, that traced the motion of the sun during the day, which the Babylonians divided into twelve parts (II 109), as now do we.

40. In 1987, Martin Bernal's *Black Athena I* collected about itself a heated controversy. Bernal's thesis was that the Greeks, led by Herodotus (p. 98 ff.), well knew that much of their civilization originated with the Egyptians, who, he claimed, were black. Ber-nal argued that the idea of a superior Greek culture, the "Aryan model," was an invention of racist latter-day Europeans who wanted to suppress the Semitic and Black origins of our culture. Aside from perpetrating a scholarly fantasy, Bernal overlooked Herodotus's distinction between origin and outcome. See below.

would I say that the Egyptians took from the Greeks . . .
any customs whatever" (II 49); the Persians adopt only
what some consider Greek vices (I 135).[41] The Scythian Anacharsis, a rare Barbarian tourist, albeit Hellenized, was killed by his own Scythian brother for being
so impressionable, so open to Greek influence (IV 77).

To me it seems that Herodotus's reports of the Egyptian and other Barbarian origins of Greek customs and
arts invoke a not-so-explicit but very deep-delving distinction between origins and outcomes. Where a practice begins does not determine what comes of it. Thus
the Greeks (of course not *the* Greeks, but certain
Greeks) took land-measuring geometry and sun-tracing
dials and putting them together, made of them astronomy, the first *science* in our sense, one of the two bases
of our modernity.[42]

The other foundation is *democracy*. In Athens, its
historical origin, opening the way to a practical political institution, is the removal of tyrants. Herodotus sets

41. Plutarch, in "The Malice of Herodotus," blames Herodotus for claiming that the Persians learned "this impurity," meaning pederasty, from the Greeks. He claims it was indigenously
Persian (13). That was the early modern view, as in Montesquieu's
Persian Letters (1721), though in the seraglio it is rather homosex-
uality than pederasty.

42. The emblematic "new science" is Copernican heliocen-
tric astronomy, based on an inversion of the Ptolemaic geocentric
hypothesis. It achieved a great mathematical simplification.

The founders of modern democracy felt themselves indebted
to the Greeks even for *representative* democracy, which would
seem to be its specifically *modern* modification (*Federalist* No. 63,
Madison or Hamilton).

this event out just where one would wish to find it: in the *center* of his history, Book V.[43] Here he says, in concluding his account and foretelling Athens' rise, that "it is clear that equal participation (*isagoria*)" in politics, the business of the city (*polis*), is a "serious asset" (V 78, more on this term below).

Having entered this reference to the Athens of Book V, which is indeed, both in position and significance, the center of the *History*—though, to be sure, not its climax—let me turn back to the last of the ethnographic books, Book IV, in which Herodotus, following, as it were, the Persian expansion, completes his Barbarian circuit by going north.

The Scythians. Beyond them live the Hyperboreans, the "Beyond-the-north-wind-ers," a semi-mythical tribe, and even beyond these is unexplored Europe (IV 13, 36, 45). These vast unknown territories enable the Scythians to vanish into an illimitable savannah.

There is a river, the Ister (Danube), which is the Nile's opposing twin, equal in length but not seasonal, a lower boundary to wide Scythia rather than a central giver of a narrow land, receiver of many lateral tributaries rather than a sole stream fanning out into a Delta.

But it is the Scythians themselves who are most tellingly opposite to the Egyptians (IV 1–82), thereby defining a Greek middle. They are largely nomadic, as

---

43. Thucydides, once again, undercuts Herodotus, crediting Sparta with putting down most of the tyrannies of Hellas and of Athens in particular (I 18); that is not how Herodotus reports it (e.g., V 62).

the Egyptians are sessile. "The greatest thing concerning all human affairs was most cleverly discovered by the Scythian race—while I don't admire them in other respects" (IV 46). This greatest and wisest contrivance prevents any attacker from escaping or overtaking them; it is their way of life. They do not farm, but drive herds; they are mounted archers, who carry their homes with them on carts. They are eminently mobile.

Who, reading this, would not think of Athens, an old town, settled around its Acropolis, a town peopled by a nation that thought of itself as "autochthonous" ("sprung from the land itself") and that had "never left its locality (*exechorese*) for anywhere else" (I 56), yet a people that was, in Themistocles' vision, reconceived as a mobile city in ships, from which its citizens could both elude the enemy and fight him (VIII 61–62).[44] Of course, Scythian oxcarts are primitive compared to Athenian triremes (the state-of-the-art square-rigged, three-tiered, oar-driven war galley with marines on board); these Athenian nautical nomads, these Themistocleans, would, had it come to that, have been a novel civic tribe, a floating *polis*.

The Scythians get high on hemp, *kannabis* (IV 75), just as the Greeks get drunk on wine (I 202, though I know of no report of Greeks doing drugs recreationally, except in the *Odyssey*[45]). These Barbarians have

44. The "Ionian" Athenians thought they were descended from the (pre-Greek) Pelasgians who were autochthonous and became Hellenized (Greek-speaking) in the (mythical) time of Ion, son of King Hellen (I 56–57, VIII 44; Thucydides I 2–3).

45. So, possibly, do the Egyptians take drugs recreationally. They eat the lotus flower whose center is like that of the poppy

interbred with Amazons; Herodotus makes a bucolic romance of this affair (IV 110–117), which seems to impugn his own report that the Scythians permit no foreign customs, since the Scythian boys readily assimilate themselves to their warrior wives (though, then again, they aren't able to learn their language). And, of course, the Scythians were partly Hellenized, as the Egyptians never were until post-Alexandrian times, and then only superficially. The semi-savage barbarians of the steppes were, perhaps, more impressionable than their hide-bound counterparts by the river. In any case, beyond the Ister, the Greeks came on tribes that were as much below them in mature cultivation as the nation of the Nile was senior to them. These roaming Scythians did first what the settled Greeks did thereafter: They thwarted the expansion of the Persian empire—by constantly harassing Darius's army and then melting away into the hinterland, until the Persian King gave up.

So NOW THAT THE barbarian periphery has circumscribed the Greeks, I return to the Persians, their most intimate opponents, as it were, especially in the person of Xerxes, who embodies what the Greeks find antithetical. The Greeks who face these Persian opponents are, in their turn, represented by leaders who, in their per-

---

(II 192). The African Lotus-eaters, who beguile Odysseus's sailors into a spacy stupor (ix 82 ff.), may be Egyptians. The Pythia of Delphi is known to have delivered her oracles from a tripod located over a rift emitting an effluvium of methane gas, but she was at work.

sons, represent their own cities' indigenous opposition and incipient antagonism.

Chief mainland battles: The battles, it falls out, display a schema, partly by historical serendipity, in the sense that they really occurred, partly by historical description, in the sense that Herodotus sees them so:

Book VI	Athens at Marathon	Miltiades vs. Darius	490
Book VII	Sparta at Thermopylae	Leonidas vs. Xerxes	480
Book VIII	Athens at Salamis	Themistocles vs. Xerxes	480
Book IX	Sparta at Plataea	Pausanias vs. Mardonius	479

Marathon is the Prelude. The Persians were already in northern Greece after the Scythian defeat, while Darius's resentment against the Athenians in particular had become a fixation; the reason was that they had aided the rebellion of their fellow Ionians in Asia Minor and had refused the king's demands. Three times at every dinner a servant was to tell him: "Zeus, grant me to punish the Athenians" (V 96ff.). Miltiades, a slippery Athenian, is the elected general at this first fending-off and defeat of the Persians on Attic soil, in which the Athenians display their characteristics: They confound the Persians by their personal agility; they charge them at a run. They are not daunted by this first encounter with men in weird Oriental dress—trousers and turbans (V 112, V 49). Besides here first encountering these aliens up close, they also experience a Spartan pattern, soon to become familiar: coming unhelpfully late for religious reasons; at Marathon the Spartans arrived in time to view the dead (VI 106, 120). Herodotus stops—as is his way—to introduce a telling bit of history: The Alcmaeonids (Pericles' family) had been accused of being in treacherous communication with the Persians; to him it is a "wonder" beyond belief, since he thinks they were true tyrant-haters and the primary liberators of Athens (VI 123). Thus Marathon is a tone-setting preview of Greek complexity: imputed deviousness and glory, suspected double dealing and freedom.

Ten years later, at Thermopylae, the Spartans are the heroes; they win by losing, and thus define an aspect of their city. By slowing down the Persian flooding of the populous part of Greece, they allow the Greeks time to get ready. The Great King is now Xerxes, who has inherited Darius's plans against Hellas, which he appropriates in his own way (see below). He is slowed in his advance into central Greece by the 298 out of 300 Spartans who sacrifice their lives at the "Hot Gates" (VII 200–238). Their king, Leonidas, one Greek untainted by corruption, is the object of Xerxes' hatred more than any other man—he brutally desecrates his corpse—not only for the humiliation of the enormous disproportion between the Spartan and the Persian dead, but also because he is simply baffled by a king who joined in the fight himself instead of looking on from a hill, as well as by his men who fought solely for honor, driven neither by the lash nor by material reward, but for a mere olive wreath (VIII 26).

The irony of this face-off is that the Spartans are now confronting Xerxes as Great King partly due to a Spartan: Demaratos, a royal who has defected to the Persian court, is said by Herodotus to have successfully argued for Xerxes' succession when Darius was deciding among his three sons, who were candidates (VII 3). This is the same Demaratos who will be Herodotus's expositor of Greek and particularly of Spartan ways to the Persians—and thus to us (VII 102 ff.). Moreover, although, or rather because, he is an expatriate, he is a particular Spartan type—a man who, once outside the discipline of Spartan custom, is peculiarly unanchored, neither here nor there. The next such, though worse in his excesses, will be Pausanias (Thucydides I 130 ff.).

Whether Thermopylae is strategically determinative, Herodotus leaves undecided. Next in this alternation of battles it is again the Athenian turn: Salamis. The Spartans had died to slow the invasion down; the Athenians will live and send Xerxes back to Persia. In a moment, I shall return to Salamis and its principal, indeed *the* hero of the *History*, Themistocles, in order to place him, as it were, between both of *his* defining counterparts, Leonidas and Pausanias.

Plataea, the concluding battle of the Persian invasion of mainland Greece, was won on the same day as Mycale, the victory degrading the Persian domination of Asian Ionia. To this battle, too, the Spartan overseas contingent arrives, as ever, late (IX 103). Herodotus reports that an encouraging rumor of the Plataean victory had flown through the ranks at Mycale—a practical impossibility; he comments that there is much proof positive of the divine being present in human affairs, of "the divinity of things," (*ta theia ton pragmaton*, IX 100). As I said, Herodotus, the ethnic differentiator, is a theological universalist: a miracle, a "thing of wonder," is not a Greek but a human event.

It is the Spartan turn to lead at Plataea; Pausanias is the general. On three occasions the Athenians yield to Spartan leadership "making the survival of Hellas the great thing" (VIII 3): first to an admiral, Eurybiades, at Artemesium, then again to the same at Salamis (VIII 42), and now to a general, Pausanias (IX 27). From the latter, they later recovered this honor because of his "hybris" (VIII 3). At Plataea they submit themselves to Spartan tactics, though in this "finest victory of all" (IX 64)—finest because conclusive—they play the major role both in individual bravery and in concerted action. A while before the battle, Mardonius, the general left in charge by Xerxes—he will fall at Plataea—had sent a message to the Athenians asking them to go over to the Persians. The Athenians invite the Spartans to be present at their resolute refusal to forego their eager defense of freedom (*eleutheria*), even in the face of the far larger Persian power. They then turn to the Spartans, chiding them for their fear that they, the Athenians, might come to an agreement with the Barbarian, though such fear "is very human." With generous courtesy, however, they assure the Spartans that

> there is neither gold enough anywhere on earth, nor any country that surpasses others so greatly in beauty and excellence which we would wish to receive, by medizing and enslaving Hellas . . . And again, it would not be well for the Athenians to become traitors to the Greek nation (*to hellenikon*)

which has the same blood and tongue as we do, and
common temples of gods and sacrifices, as well as the
same kind of customs (VIII 144).

And then, very politely but pertinently, they ask Sparta
to be a "little beforehand in coming to help" in Boeotia, that is, to Plataea. In the event, the Spartans daw-
dle again over a festival and the building of a wall across
the Peloponnesian isthmus, until the Persians retake the
Acropolis. The Athenians feel betrayed.

This, to my mind the most magnificent speech in the
History, will resonate in Herodotus's last paragraph,
which is, I have claimed, a warning to the post-Persian
Athenians against intemperance. This Athenian generation, the "great generation" of Herodotus's—and, indeed, of Greece's—history, refuses the chief temptation
of winners, to suppose that "they should grasp for more,"
(*pleonos oregonto*, Thucydides IV 21).

But back to Pausanias, the general of Plataea. During the time span of Plataea, he shows himself to be a
moderate, humane, disciplined Spartan, even witty in
the "laconic" Spartan mode. He had captured Xerxes'
sumptuously furnished tent, which the King left to Mardonius. Pausanias ordered the cooks to prepare a Persian
banquet and then told his own servants to produce one
of those famously spare and unattractive Laconian meals
of black blood broth. When the suppers were ready, he
laughed and invited the Greek leadership to this dual
dinner to show them the Persians' senselessness in coming, with such a lifestyle, to "deprive us of our misery"
(IX 82). This, too, resonates in the final paragraph of

the *History*, interpreted above as a warning, particularly
to the Athenians (because they are the ones Herodotus
most cares about), not to be tempted to engage in conquest for the sake of rich living or domination.

But shortly after, now the admiral of the Spartan
navy, Pausanias went corrupt. Violent, oppressive, luxurious—he kept, irony of ironies, a Persian table and
wore Median costume. He enters into clandestine relations with Xerxes and finally dies ignominiously, starved
to death in a Spartan sanctuary to which he had fled.
The Spartans do not replace him for fear of seeing another man similarly deteriorate. This sorry aftermath is
told by Thucydides in *The Peloponnesian War* (I 94 ff.,
129 ff.). He also tells us that Pausanias's bad behavior
was a chief reason why the Greek allies turned to the
Athenians (I 130). And that, of course, was the cause
of the Peloponnesian War, a civil rather than a national
war, a tragic time and the end of Athens' grandeur. For,
it seems, a history must be unlike a tragedy, among other
features, in this: The latter, whether it ends in triumph
or catastrophe for its hero, comes off as elevating. Aristotle says that spectators of tragic drama (which falls
"within one circuit of the sun") leave purified by pity
and fear (*Poetics* 1449b).[46] In contrast, history, that is,
reality written up (which has no time limit), must often
follow a descending curve into mere decline and an ultimate loss which has really, unredeemably, come about.
That is a history's showing-forth. Herodotus was lucky
to be able to end on a high note, but as I claimed, he had

46. Though could that be said of Euripidean melodramas?

forebodings and also foreknowledge, since he is thought to have lived through the first decade of the civil war. Of Athens' fate he had only surmises, but of Pausanias's corruption he surely had knowledge—and this thought gives a, probably intended, ironic meaning to the Pausanian dinner anecdote.

Thucydides couples, as I am about to, Pausanias with Themistocles: "Such were the ends of Pausanias the Lacedaemonian and Themistocles the Athenian, the most famous Hellenes of their time" (Thucydides I 138). For Themistocles too had laid himself open to a charge of Medism and had to flee, having already been ostracized from Athens,[47] to the Persians. Their king was by then Xerxes' son, Artaxerxes, who is named by Herodotus in connection with that Delian earthquake mentioned earlier, the one he thought portended the evils of civil war to befall Greece during Artaxerxes' reign (VI 98).

Thucydides quotes a letter from Themistocles to Artaxerxes, asking to be received at court, in which he mentions his behavior at Salamis, presenting it, cunningly, as pro-Persian (I 137); I am about to come to Salamis. Then Themistocles does something Greeks were as unlikely to do as modern Americans: He learns Persian. And then he flees to Persia and becomes an influential advisor—imagine!—on the enslaving of Greece, evidently not yet a dead hope with Xerxes' son. Them-

---

47. People were ostracized, sent into exile, sometimes for very trivial reasons, by popular vote scratched on pottery sherds (*ostraka*). Thucydides gives no reason for Themistocles' ostracism (I 134).

istocles died of illness in exile, and his bones were secretly brought home to Athens at his request. It was not
a noble demise, but it was not ignominious either, being
perfectly in character, a character, like Odysseus's—
beyond nobility, though not below dignity. Thucydides
writes his obituary as an encomium:

> In the year he kept his distance, he learned as much
> of the Persian language as he could and the customs
> of the land; and arriving after the one year, he became
> important in his [the king's] court to a degree that no
> other Hellene had, both because of his established rep-
> utation and because of the hope he offered him of en-
> slaving Hellas, but above all from demonstrations of
> his manifest intelligence. For Themistokles, display-
> ing the very surest signs of natural ability, was far and
> away more worthy than anyone else of admiration for
> this quality. By native intelligence, without preparing
> or supplementing it by study, he was with the briefest
> deliberation the most effective in decisions about im-
> mediate situations and the best at conjecturing what
> would happen farthest into the future; whatever he was
> engaged in he was capable of explaining, over matters
> in which he had no experience he was not incapacitated
> from judging adequately, and in particular he foresaw
> what better or worse possibilities were still concealed
> in the future. To sum up, this man by natural ability,
> with rapid deliberation, was certainly supreme in his
> immediate grasp of what was necessary.[48]

48. Thucydides, *The Peloponnesian War* I 138, trans. by Ste-
ven Lattimore, Hackett Publishing (1998).

I cite Thucydides because it is helpful to my sense that Themistocles is the living hero of Herodotus's *History* to have the post-mortem corroboration of his stature by so sober a historian—and an Athenian. What is missing in the memorial is mention of his superb Attic audacity[49] and his ultimate Athenian patriotism, lately occulted—for which dimming he had some cause.

Here is Herodotus's account of this man, at the center of which is the third of the great engagements, the Athenian battle, namely the naval engagement at Salamis. Themistocles is presented as "newly arrived; his name was called Themistocles, the child (*pais*) of Neocles" (VII 143). It is an arresting locution; in contrast, Leonidas, the hero of Thermopylae, a king of long lineage, is, as is normal, called Leonidas "of Anaxandridas" (VII 204). It is as if Herodotus were drawing attention to the father's name: "New-famed," and suppressing his not undistinguished Lycomid ancestry.[50] He was, one might say, Themistocles "of Athens." An anecdote confirms this: An otherwise unknown Athenian kept, out of envy, deprecating the prizes bestowed on Themistocles in Sparta (always a recourse for unappreciated Athenians, as later for Alcibiades[51]), because they came to him only through his being from Athens, not through himself. Quick as ever, Themistocles replied,

49. Thucydides himself reports a case of Themistocles' audacious deception on behalf of Athens, not much later than the one at Salamis that I am about to tell of; this time directed against the enemy-to-be, Sparta (I 191).

50. *Landmark Herodotus*, note on VII 143.

51. Thucydides VI 88.

"This is how it is: If I had been a Belbinian [Belbina is a nothing-island off Attica] I wouldn't have been so honored by the Spartiates, nor would you, though you're an Athenian" (VIII 125). Themistocles means this: Being Athenian is a necessary but not sufficient cause of my excellence; being myself completes the condition.

Readers—I have heard this myself—will come away with the sense that Herodotus is ambivalent or even negative about this ever-clever, cunning newcomer. (After all, he is a great admirer of some of the older noble families, like the Alcmaeonids, VI 123–125.) Among those readers is Plutarch, in "The Malice of Herodotus," which I mentioned earlier.[52] He claims that Herodotus slanders Themistocles by presenting him as a despoiler of treasure and a thief of ideas, and subverts his role in

---

52. Plutarch was a Boeotian; in the *History*, the Boeotians are infamous "Medizers," the Persian-collaborating quislings of the war. Hence his resentment. An earlier, greater Boeotian, the Theban poet Pindar, testifies in a different spirit to Athens' role in resisting the Persians everywhere:

> Oh, the glistening and the violet-crowned and the much sung
> *Prop of Hellas*, famous Athens, miraculous city!

And for the sea battle at Artemesium in particular:

> . . . where the sons of Athens laid the bright foundation of freedom.

Both fragments come from hymns dated to 474. The Thebans are said to have fined Pindar a thousand drachmas for these praise songs to Athens; the Athenians rewarded him with ten thousand and a statue.

Whoever has seen Hymettos, the backdrop-mountain of Athens, go purple at sunset can envision her as "violet-crowned" (*iostephanoi*).

the battle of Salamis (37). Plutarch, incidentally, reports that the Greeks gave Themistocles the epithet of "Odysseus" for his "ingenuity" (*phronesis*, 38)—and having in mind, I imagine, that their goddess Athena was also Odysseus's own divinity and even admiring friend: for being such a liar! (*Odyssey* xiii 287 ff.)

The Herodotean Themistocles performs two major services for his city. First, with the aid of a clever interpretation of an oracle, he causes Athens to rely on the navy that he had been instrumental in building and that would be her refuge and salvation; second, by a risky, daring deceit, he forces the sea engagement at Salamis, which first begins to turn the Persian tide. Cleverness shading into deceit, lying sustained by wisdom, ingenious audacity: that describes him.[53]

The Delphic priestess's defeatist oracle had been amended, under pressure, to be more helpful. The new version spoke of a "wooden wall" granted by Zeus to Athena, a wall that would profit her and her children (VII 141). Some people thought that the wall meant a thorn hedge which had once enclosed the Acropolis. It is here that Themistocles first comes on the scene with an interpretation in line with his previous shipbuilding designs (VII 143–144). Its aim was to encourage those people who thought that the "wooden walls" meant their navy.

The deceit at Salamis is mouth-droppingly audacious and hair-raisingly risky. The allies, assembled under a

---

53. Herodotus, as Thucydides after him, has more reports of Themistocles' ruses, devices, and briberies, which I omit here.

Spartan admiral, are about to retreat behind the wall they have been building across the isthmus into the Peloponnesus. Themistocles sends a private servant to tell the investing Persians that the terrified Greeks are about to flee. The Persians close in on Salamis during the night. Their own crews go felicitously sleepless, and the next morning the rested Greeks are nailed to the place of their victory. The news is brought by Aristeides, who is at that very moment returning from his ostracism—apparently imposed for being insufferably virtuous; his epithet was "the Just."[54] Aristeides had called out his old political antagonist, Themistocles, from a heated meeting and told him of the Persian action. Themistocles trusted him with an account of his trick and asked him to announce the situation (VIII 74 ff.). The most scrupulously honest and the most unscrupulously cunning of Athenians colluded in a kind of loyal treason for the saving of what Herodotus calls *to hellenikon*, "the Hellenic [nation]" (VIII 144). It is an irony that will not have eluded Herodotus; the Hellenic nation is particularly productive of irony (meaning the poignant incongruity of events), because of its built-in enmities and oppositions. But Herodotus's appreciation of irony is comple-

---

54. Plutarch, *Aristeides*. There is "a familiar story" in which Aristeides is asked by an illiterate fellow citizen to scratch his own name on an *ostrakon*, a pot-sherd; the man, asked why, says "I am tired of hearing him called 'Aristeides the Just'" (*The Illustrated London News*, Oct. 19, 1935, p. 645.). His justness, this unblemished uprightness, makes Aristeides in character what he was indeed in politics—Themistocles' antagonist *par excellence*. But he turns up only at Salamis in Herodotus's *History*.

mented by the straightforward candor of his reverence:[55]
He says that he cannot call into question an oracular
response, or be receptive to those who do so, when presented with one so prescient as to foretell that, when
Ares will redden the sea with blood, then will "Hellas
see the day of freedom" (VIII 77). Call this naiveté who
will; to me it seems proper awe at truth foretold.

One defining opposition for Themistocles comes from
the side of the Spartan duo, Leonidas of Thermopylae,
the courageous and steadfast king, and Pausanias of Plataea (Leonidas's nephew, IX 64), the corruptible and un-
stable regent. Against these two, Themistocles shows
forth as both daring and flexible, a man not of unbudg-
ing last-ditch tactics nor of collapse in the face of success, but of chance-taking resourcefulness, who has
a head and keeps it, but above all, who is not depen-
dent on being among his own for what we would call his
"identity," his self-sameness, but a man who is everywhere *himself* and everywhere *an Athenian*—both.[56]
What makes the two Spartans the men they are I will try
to set out below, when I sketch Herodotus's view of their
city. For Themistocles, an ethnographic account cannot

55. There is a non-committal irony, romantic irony, that oscil-
lates between determinate allegiances (set out in Søren Kierkegaard's *Concept of Irony*, 1841, "Tieck") and another irony that
plays in the ether of devotion, appreciative of serendipity, that of
Herodotus.

56. Hence his similarity to Odysseus, who, though Agamem-
non's prop at Troy, is above all Penelope's husband, Telemachus's
father, and Ithaca's king, wherever he wanders—and always
Odysseus.

cover the phenomenon of the man, since for this Athenian, "custom is king" does not hold—and yet he is altogether an Athenian, a man whose city is, by reason of its customs, "the Hellenic [nation]" incarnate and *par excellence*. It comes near being a paradox, an enigma.

As Themistocles is defined as an Athenian by comparison to the Spartan leaders, so the Hellene nation is brought into relief by the Persians, as personified in the Great King—though Xerxes is perhaps not really their "personification" (since no Persian is like him), but rather so to speak, in a "mutual projection" with them: Their slavery is the counter-image of his despotism, and his tyranny is the concretion of their subservience.

And so finally the Persians of the Orient, their empire on the brink of its greatest expansion, a multifarious mass, compliant to any command, unsustainable by any logistics, begin to roll into the European West under their King, to face the Greeks, a tiny, diverse nation, mainly recalcitrant to submission and at home in a sparse land.

The King, on the throne by inheritance, is a slave-master, a despot, unlike Cyrus, who is a king by nature, a truly royal, a wise king. Herodotus in fact depicts in Xerxes a tyrant as the Greeks came to understand that term, and much as we do. His warrant for this portrayal is that he thinks of the Persians as having a polity, a civic framework in the Greek mode. After the palace coup that led to the accession of Darius, Herodotus relates, a remarkable discussion took place among the three conspirators, which, he says, some Greeks think never happened—"but it did"(III 80). I think it didn't but that it doesn't much matter. This Greek view of the Persian debate prefigures developed Greek political philosophy in recognizing three main forms of government and one of the three related degenerate forms: democracy, oligarchy, and monarchy—rule of the many, the people, of the few, the wealthy, and of the one, the wise king—and tyranny as a *bad*, debased monarchy (III 81).[57] Darius, the defender of monarchy among the three contenders, wins, and in winning lays the predicate for his son's tyranny. That, to be sure, is the last we hear of political discussion among the Persians. When Xerxes, in the next generation, is told of the Spartan polity, he is simply nonplussed.

I should say that in general "tyranny" means a one-man rule instituted by force or guile, (often upon a degenerated democracy) unlimited by law and ending in wanton outrage. "There is nothing more unjust or

57. Compare Plato, *Republic* VIII; Aristotle, *Politics* III 7. The Greek poets sometimes use "tyrant" in an older sense to mean simply "king," as in the title of Sophocles' *Oedipus Tyrannus*, and in line 128. Though perhaps there is an overtone of illegitimacy; in line 873 the perjorative sense is plain.

In the conspirators' discussion, "democracy" is not the term used, but *isonomia*, "equality before the law" (see *Landmark Herodotus*, note on III 80); similarly, *isokratia*, "equal power" (V 92).

The first Median (pre-Persian) king, Deioces, turns his kingship into a tyranny by becoming inaccessible. He builds Ecbatana, a fortress city, with massive concentric walls, each of a different color: white, black, crimson, dark blue, orange, and plated with gold and silver (I 98). In the dialogue *Critias*, Plato delineates Atlantis, a techno-tyranny whose concentric walls are similarly designed; I imagine Herodotus provided the model.

bloodstained among men," says a Corinthian trying to dissuade the Spartans from moving to reinstitute a former tyranny in Athens (V 92).

Back in Persia, upon legitimately succeeding his father, Darius, Xerxes still displays some imagination and pliability. He has—misleadingly—prophetic dreams, is undecided, and takes advice. But even on the way from Susa to Greece, he develops a capricious cruelty (VII 39).

At the Hellespont, as he is about to cross into European Greece, he commits four revealing acts. He has a pontoon bridge built, thus connecting Asia and Europe and in effect shackling the river. (To Herodotus and probably to Xerxes, the strait we call the Dardanelles was a river, VII 35.) When it is wrecked in a storm, he beheads the supervisors of the construction and has the river whipped with three hundred lashes, while it is insulted with words and a pair of actual shackles is thrown into it (VII 35). Recall that this act of domination is being perpetrated by a Persian, whose ancestral customs include the worship of rivers; it is a blasphemous outrage. Later the bridge is rebuilt—a marvel of engineering—and Xerxes, after praying to the sun to conquer Europe to the limits, in short, to acquire the inhabited world of the West, propitiates the river with golden gifts (VII 54).

Second, before his army crosses, he seats himself on a hill and, self-congratulatingly, reviews his enormous force. Then he bursts into tears, and when asked the reason, says that he was suddenly overcome by pity: "How brief is every human life, so that none of these many people will be alive a hundred years from now"

(VII 46). This from a feckless leader of a force that is drinking the rivers dry, can't live off the land (as he has been told, VII 48), and is clearly slated for decimation by hardship and battle! This from a slave-driving king whose army goes into battle under the lash (VII 55) and will die by myriads![58] This sentimental weeping is a queasy-making, semi-sentiment, the crocodile tears of the heartless.

A third act will come later, after the defeat of Salamis, when Xerxes leaves his generals on their own and runs home to Susa (VIII 100 ff.). Perhaps a king sometimes has a prerogative, even a sober duty, of self-preservation for reasons of state, for his people. But this is undignified skedaddling, a lily-livered shrinking from seeing it through. These acts display Xerxes in turn as arrogantly blasphemous, heedlessly sentimental, and irresponsibly self-centered, a complex that delineates a tyrannical soul—one without due reverence for the powers above, and without attentive feeling to fellow-humanity, without effective loyalty to underlings.

Add to this picture a fourth act, which reveals an absence of self-control within the family: Herodotus's last

58. In modern times, neither Napoleon nor Hitler, driven by reckless expansionism, shrank from taking huge armies into inhospitable territory—though Russia was insuperable because of its harsh illimitableness (recall Herodotus's Scythia) while Greece had been resistant because of its invigorating constrictedness. You can't profit from history if you don't know how to adapt it to your own circumstances; that, however, demands so much acute calibration as to invoke the suspicion that it might be simpler to bypass history and judge the present afresh—precisely Themistocles' genius.

notice of Xerxes, very close to the end of the *History*, shows him and his wife in Susa embroiled in repellently indecent, brutally conducted, erotic intrigues (IX 109–113), and that is his final report of the Great King.[59] I have no doubt that Herodotus means here to top off his portrayal of the tyrant in-the-flesh by giving us a close-up, a vignette of his personal affairs.

This king leads a motley crew against the ethnically diverse Greeks. However, for all their colorful mul-tifariousness, the Persian forces meld into a malleable mass, precisely because they are polyglot and thus ef-fectively incommunicado, while by then even the once-free Persians themselves are without a tradition of liberty (IX 122).[60] The Greeks, on the other hand, are never really mergeable, except for brief moments when their Hellenic nationality emerges. They know how to use the language they have in common to drive them-selves apart. (Recall Churchill's description of Britain and America as two peoples divided by a common lan-guage.) But they are not driven to battle; on the con-trary, they divide into the coalition of the willing (who are sometimes tempted to treason) and the unwilling (whose Medizing is often uncertain).

Xerxes cannot catch on at all, as I noted. He has with him that exiled quondam-king, the Spartan Demaratus, who tries to give him lessons: The Spartans at Thermo-

59. "Great King" is first used by Herodotus of Cyrus (I 88, later V 49, et al.).

60. In any case, for the Asians escaping slavery seems to mean liberation from foreign domination—national independence, rather than personal freedom.

pylae will fight against his overwhelming numbers, "for they are free but not altogether free, since there is a despot over them—the Law, of which they stand in secret awe far more than your people do of you" (VII 104). Xerxes laughs. He remains unconvinced by Demaratus's explanations and prognoses, then and later (VII 103–105, 209).

Now this secretly feared law (*nomos*) of the Spartans is an inward ordinance, not a written law but one taken in, learned "by heart" from word of mouth. The memorial distych (two-liner) by Simonides, set up at Thermopylae, speaks of *rhemata*, the "words," the oral ordinances, in obedience to which they died (VII 228):

> Stranger, tell them in Sparta that here
> We lie, obedient to their words.

Leonidas, the king who does not view the battle from a throne but dies leading it, is the incarnation of this poignantly concise verse. He sends the not-so-willing allies away from this suicidal mission so as to sequester all the glory for the three-hundred "Spartiates" (the Spartans proper); the main Spartan force was, as usual, delayed by the celebration of a festival (VII 206, 221, 220). Watching Leonidas's sort of kingship makes the Great King savage (VII 238).

Obedience to unwritten and internalized law is both the strength and weakness of Sparta. Such law is indeed custom, that is, a second nature, immediately and spontaneously operative, but it needs continual reinforce-

ment from the hearing of its precepts and by the sight
of its practice; it requires living in its community. Pausanias is an example of a Spartan away from Sparta;
his learned-by-heart discipline is just as fugitive as mere
memory can be under temptation.[61]

The Spartans are actually complex and endangered
characters. They complement their constitutional pro-
crastination in marching out of Sparta with a quick wit
and an ingenious practicality. And they live with sup-
pressions—of dark things, like their brutality to their
serfs, the helots,[62] and of lighter ones, like their suppres-
sion of intellect in favor of wit; they are, on occasion,
grave, but never deep. Their wisdom is not their individual own but that of their "common meals," their *syssitia*,
instituted by Lycurgus (I 65). Perhaps more accurately, if
they have questions about the nature of things—which,
I believe, is a universal human propensity—they don't
let them rise to expression. But that leaves them, under
the onslaught of alien temptation, without the support
of the self-sustaining judgment, which would come not
from a custom-shaped, brittle character but from a re-
silient, thought-governed inner life. In this sense Pausanias, is, revealingly, a Spartan with a Spartan fate.

And Themistocles is his revealing opposite—compara-
ble not just because he is the hero of the penultimate battle of Salamis, the victory at sea, paired by history (that
ex post facto oracle of fate) with Plataea, the conclusion
on land, but also because, like Pausanias, Themistocles

61. Plutarch, *Lycurgus* para. 27.
62. Ibid. para. 28.

ends up in discord with his city and in intrigues with the reigning Persian king—and because Thucydides thinks of them as a pair. But Themistocles shaped his exile with some success; he proceeded with shrewdness and self-control, and after a full life his end, though less noble than that of Leonidas, was far less pathetic than that of Pausanias.

Not noble but bold, not fragile but flexible, not habit-set but self-aware: not Spartan but Athenian—that is Themistocles, "called the child of Neocles." Herodotus paints him neither as a distinctively individualized Athenian (he is much less a person than his Odyssean avatar) nor as your lowest-common-denominator Athenian (such as Aristophantic characters present). Instead he is, in his very distinctiveness, an *ethnic type*,[63] a sketch of a being with features not necessarily either ideal or universal, and nonetheless recognizable as Athena's Athens personified, as an embodied epitome—an ethnographer's schema—and that paradox, a singular type.[64]

---

63. *Ethnos*, which gives us our adjective "ethnic," is pervasive in the *History*. It is used of the Barbarians both in the singular and the plural (I 4), of the Greeks in the singular (e.g., I 4; VIII 144) where as often it is not written, but understood: *to hellenikon* [*ethnos*]. Therefore it means the largest human division, that into Greek and Barbarian, and also tribe, people, nation. The word *typos* (from *typtein*, "to strike"), whence "type," means "stamped impression" or "carved figure." Herodotus does not use it as we do, for a human type (J.E. Powell, *A Lexicon to Herodotus*, Hildesheim: Olms, 1966).

64. Giambattista Vico, in his *New Science* (1744), presents a poetic mode, the "imaginative universal," a condensation of all the appearances of a specific character-set into a named hero; thus

The national feature he incarnates is set out in the first book of the *History* and in a most telling context, Herodotus's astonished discovery that these Athenians can be naïve: Their ousted tyrant, Peisistratus, is trying to regain power (in the mid-sixth century) and succeeds with a trick which, Herodotus says, was the most naïve affair by far that he ever discovered (I 60),[65] particularly so since

> of old the Hellenic nation has been distinguished from the Barbarian nation as being the shrewdest and quite free of silly naiveté, and, moreover, because these people [the Peisistratids] then worked such a device (*mechanontai*) on the Athenians who were said to be first among the Hellenes in discernment.[66]

Odysseus is the reduction (in the culinary sense) of prudence. The Herodotean type, however, is not imaginatively poetic but ethnographically descriptive. Yet it is like Vico's in being a *many-in-one*, since surely many Athenians were a bit like the *one-and-only* Themistocles.

65. The tyrant's party found a very tall and beautiful woman whom they dressed in armor, set in a chariot and drove into the city, announcing that Athena herself was bringing back Peisistratus, the deposed tyrant. Some citizens were taken in—the substandard intellects found even among the Athenians.

66. "Discernment," cleverness: *sophia*. Later on it means wisdom, theoretical or practical. For Herodotus, it may mean skill, that is, craft in the good sense, or craftiness, trickery, and sometimes, as I think, above, discernment. "Sophist" still means a sage (I 29); later, among the philosophers, it denominates a paid knowledge-monger.

Herodotus declares that Athens saved Hellas (VII 139) and, by introducing Themistocles after this declaration, implies that Themistocles saved the Athenians; his most spectacular deed being his stealthy gamble in inviting the Persians to close off the Greek fleet's retreat at Salamis. It seems to me that readers who have ever served in a command position must ask themselves whether they would have had the nerve for it. If it had failed it would have meant disgrace and death for him—and defeat for his city.

This might be the moment to draw Herodotus into another imaginative exercise. Salamis sent the Persian king back to Susa, but not the Persian army—a great land battle was yet required. But think of the other possibility: If the Greeks had lost here or had scattered south to cover their Isthmus with its futile "cloak of walls" (VII 139), the Persians would surely have marched by land into Laconia[67] and sailed to Cythera, an island crucial to Spartan security, which Democritus had earlier advised Xerxes (who, as usual, rejected the good counsel) to take in order to attack Sparta from the sea (Thucydides IV 53, Herodotus VII 235).

What great and wonderful works would then have come to be in Europe and its America? Probably not these: science and democracy. For the Persian bequest to Europe, the one that would have aborted the Greek legacy we actually live off,[68] would have been the religion,

67. Laconia; the region of which Sparta was the capital.
68. Because it kick-started our modernity.

not the science, of nature, and the institution of despotism, not of freedom.

Herodotus's Themistocles appears to me, then, as a first and a fixating incarnation of a man of democratic freedom. Here is some evidential data: He isn't particularly low-born but appears as a newcomer. He is shrewdly provident, persuading the Greeks to appropriate the income from their silver-mines to building a navy by cannily interpreting an oracle one way which he will later interpret another way.[69] Apparently, he is the inventor of political propaganda, scratching messages on rocks to persuade the Medizers to defect (VIII 23). He accepts and dispenses bribes in pursuit of his political purposes (VIII 4–5). And he has no scruples about appropriating good advice as his own (VIII 57).[70] This litany sounds unsavory, but in fact it's the first instance of real democratic politics—practical intelligence (glossed as prudence in the high, craftiness in the low view) applied patriotically in the cause of a city that is the freest of the inhabited world, and yet also nationally, in behalf of the Hellenic nation with which Athens feels herself, beyond all the differences, at one in essentials: consanguinity, common language, common sacred rituals, common customs. These are, as well, all the elements of that great Athenian speech (VIII 143) cited above,

---

69. The oracle of the "wooden walls" (VII 141) is made to mean first: Prepare for a sea fight and do not abandon Attica to settle elsewhere (VII 143). And later: Prepare to board your ships to sail for Italy (VIII 62).

70. Plutarch imputes this to him for malice (37).

which I would bet was fittingly composed by Themistocles and willingly recited by the Athenian spokesmen. In
this same address they speak of themselves as "eagerly
struggling for freedom (*eleutheries glichomenoi*). And
indeed, the history of the Athenians, which Herodotus sets out in his middle book, the fifth, is largely the
confused struggle against their own tyrants.[71] These *de
facto* rulers, though not always tyrannical in the degenerate way of Xerxes, were surely not supporters of *isagoria*—Herodotus's word for democracy, meaning "equal
in assembly." It is from *isos*, "equal," and *ageirein*, "to
gather," hence *agoreuein* "to speak in public or in assembly." The *agora*, the venue for gatherings, is the marketplace, where citizens gather to buy, sell, and talk,
which, as mentioned above, Cyrus despises as a place
of deceit (I 153). Deceit is—Herodotus's Cyrus is surely
right—endemic to any place where people gather freely
and speak freely, freedom being the realm of truth *and*
its other. For *isagoria* connotes both freedom of assembly (different voices) and freedom of speech (true and
not-so-true).[72]

71. This is the development with which Thucydides wants to
credit Sparta (I 18).

72. The Athenian Agora was, in fact, the center of civic activity—though the legislative Assembly had moved from the Agora
to the Pnyx, (a hill ten minutes' walk from the Agora), evidently
just before the Persian occupations of 480–479 (*The Athenian
Agora: A Guide to the Excavation and Museum*, 1962, p. 22; also
Mabel Lang, *The Athenian Citizen: Democracy in the Athenian
Agora*, 2004, p. 6 [both published by the American School of Classical Studies at Athens]).

Right near the middle of the middle book—I think he is marking by position the crux of his *History*—Herodotus breaks in with an opinion:

> So now the Athenians flourished, and it is clear, not only in one but in every way, that *isagoria* is a serious asset [*spoudaion chrema*]. Though the Athenians, when under tyrants, were not better in matters of war than any whatsoever of the people living around them, yet, once relieved of tyrants, they were first by far. Thus it is clear that while they were repressed they malingered [*ethelokakeon*, "were intentionally base"], since they were working for a despot, but once having gained their freedom, each one was inspirited to work for himself (V 78).

Thus Herodotus has now added individualism to a propensity for freedom of association and speech, and this, together with the ethnic Athenian intelligence earlier noted, surely describes the conditions and ingredients of the Themistoclean type—and ours when most ourselves.

As I said, shining Leonidean nobility is not much in evidence. After Salamis the Greek commanders tried to choose the bravest and noblest, the *aristos*, or best, the man of greatest excellence in this war. Every Greek voted for himself first and second for Themistocles. And so they sailed off, the prize unawarded (I 123). To me it makes sense: Aside from the exigencies of individualistic self-esteem, Themistocles' contribution does not belong first—or perhaps anywhere—in a ranking for traditional *aristeia* (I 123), the prize given for Homeric-type bravery, for "furious valor." His genius was for competent foresight and composed fortitude—a daring that had too much of the clever maneuver, too much of the cunning intellect about it to win a public competition for *honor.* Though I would not have voted for myself[73] (because we don't do that kind of thing except in secret ballot), I would not have voted for Themistocles either, especially if I had known of his ruse (as the voting warriors presumably did not). I would have thought that he was the goddess's gift to Athens, made in her own and her city's image, but more deserving of the central spot in a history still to be written than of a solemn celebration on the site of his victory.

Yet, as commander of the Athenian navy (Thucydides I 74), he was certainly on board and, I imagine, urging on his men to good effect, just as his diametric opposite and duped antagonist, the Great King, was ensconced on land, putting the fear of their lord in the sailors who thought themselves watched by him—and

73. In this sea battle, a woman—the queen under whom Herodotus was born, Artemesia—was both a sensible advisor to a king who rarely, as I've said, took good advice, and his most ruthlessly daring commander (VII 99, VIII 87). Xerxes says of her, "My men have become women, the women men" (VIII 88).

A thought on singular cases, such as Artemesia's: While they don't disprove *general* judgments about the unsuitableness of women as warriors, they do nullify *generic* judgments; one exception disproves the universal, as one (genuinely) intellectual chimp would erase the chief species distinction between us and animals. In any case, Herodotus already knows about the Amazons (IV 110 ff., IX 27).

thereby really wreaking havoc (VIII 86, 89–90). One might say that Xerxes ruled by calling on the force of fear to drive his slaves, Themistocles by calling up the force of circumstance to compel his fellow-citizens.

So he is a man not so much of moral as of intellectual virtue, in the terms Aristotle would later use (*Nicomachean Ethics* 1103 a). The moral virtue he does possess—his diplomatic willingness to yield rank and power—is un-heroic and somewhat more apt to be admired by us than by the Athenians. At the insistence of their allies the Athenians had ceded to Sparta the admiralship of the Greek navy, although more than half of its ships were Athenian. This was at Artemisium, a first sea battle, aborted by a storm. Themistocles was there, and in fact bribed the Spartan admiral, Eurybiades, not to flee. From this I infer that he had been in line for the high command, participated in the highest counsels, and was responsible for the Athenian thinking behind this concession: "They made the survival of Hellas the great thing, knowing that if they quarreled about the leadership, Hellas would perish." Herodotus adds: "and they thought correctly" (VIII 3 ff.). Of course, at Salamis too, not Themistocles but Eurybiades was admiral (VIII 42). At Plataea as well, the generalship was ceded to the Spartan Pausanias. It is pure speculation, but this compliant generosity in the face of an overarching interest may have been a Themistoclean legacy.[74]

---

74. Themistocles was evidently not at Plataea and does not appear in the ninth, the final book of the *History*. Right after

What redeems Themistocles from mere brilliance—an attribute not by itself sufficient for greatness—and puts him among the "great and wonderful" phenomena that Herodotus is memorializing, is the pervasive, underlying feeling that informs his canny counseling[75] and supports his bold machinations: his love of "the Hellenic [nation]" with its single language and common customs, amid which his Athens had come into being and which she in time overtopped. So this Athenian Odysseus is like his model not only in being a versatile man "of many turns" (*Odyssey* I 1), but also, as the Homeric Odysseus never met a woman he couldn't (and wouldn't) charm, yet was, even in his wanderings, true husband only to one, Penelope, so Themistocles, who could make himself useful anywhere (and did), was a true citizen of Athens to the last.[76]

I have meant to show that Herodotus's "showing-forth" (*apodexis*) of his history (*historia*) has a double intention. Its lesser but requisite element, no doubt sus-

---

Salamis he was operating around the Aegean islands, extorting money and reinforcing his intrigues with the Great King (VIII 109, 112); shortly after Plataea he organized the clandestine fortification of Athens—activities that were a mixture of protection of self and defense of the city (Thucydides I 90 ff.).

75. Plutarch reports that he provoked the later, anyhow inevitable, ostracism mentioned above by building near his house a temple to Artemis "of the Best Advice," implying—rightly—that he was the best counselor in Greece.

76. Themistocles' bones were, as I mentioned, by his wishes brought home to Athens and there secretly buried (Thucydides I 138).

tained by his zestful curiosity, is to preserve the great and wonderful works of the whole inhabited world from the oblivion that time brings. The grander and intellectually more demanding plan is, by the fruits of his foreign inquiries, to paint a picture of that world as containing two great antithetical constituents, Greeks and Barbarians, and to write the history of their antagonism. Although he aims his inquiry, his "history," aetiologically at the cause of their recent war, he shapes it ethnographically as an encompassing, comprehensive, and, so to speak, comprehending schema—one of concertedly encircling antitheses.[77] In pursuit of this design he visits and delineates the environing Barbarians, both because they are wonderful in themselves and because it is in opposition to them that the thus pin-pointed Greeks are to be defined.[78] When the Greeks have actually, in battles with real dates, engaged with and expelled the Persians, who are their most particular and, as it were, most inti-

---

77. I am averse to putting the following reflection in the text and reluctant to omit it: Among the most consequential notions of Western metaphysics is the identity of delimiting Nonbeing with diversifying Otherness (Plato, *Sophist* 258 b). I think of the *History* as its grandly *concrete forerunner*.

A second such reflection: I have come to think of the great Greeks—Homer, Herodotus, Socrates—as having this common and probably *defining characteristic*: openness to wonders *and* to wondering.

78. More and more, Tocqueville seems to me Herodotus's modern counterpart, a young traveler of immense powers of observant insight, visiting the wondrous American Barbarians to gather an understanding of Europe's fate. And no one can tell: Is he explorer, ethnographer, political scientist—or the interpreter of providential divinity?

mate Barbarians, then, as in Cavafy's poem, left in the
lurch by relief, they allow their own internally defining
antitheses to shape up ever more ominously into antago-
nisms. Now it is the rivalry with Sparta that puts Athens
at the center of a Greece which is the center of the inhabited world—at the center of the center that Herodotus has "shown forth" in his *History*'s one thousand
five hundred and thirty-four paragraphs. It is, as I said,
roughly at the literal center of the *History* that Herodotus inserts his encomium of Athenian freedom (V 78),
but by the end he has issued warnings of Athenian empire as well.

Herodotus's love of all works great and wonderful does, to be sure, load the *History* with much detail,
some of which contributes only indirectly to the organizing schema, though it fleshes out the supporting ethnography. By and large, the intellectual diagram that I
think I see really does absorb the so-called digressions
and excursuses, tales and anecdotes, into one comprehensive intention, which from its early approaches to its
final culmination means finally to converge on one place,
Athens—or better, one people, who *might* form a city
even without a place. Just before the three great battles
of 480–479 and just before he brings Themistocles on
the scene, and right after mentioning an act of degener-
ating Athenian morality perpetrated fifty years later (VII
137, Thucydides II 67), he interrupts his account to say:

> Here I am driven by necessity to show forth a judg-
> ment that will incur the hatred of a good many peo-
> ple, but from which I will not refrain since it seems

to me true. If the Athenians, terrified of the danger coming upon them, had abandoned their own [city], or, not abandoning but remaining in it had delivered themselves over to Xerxes, no one would have tried to oppose the King by sea. If, now, no one had opposed Xerxes by sea, then by land the following would have come about: even if many cloaks [*chitones*] of wall had been thrown across the Isthmus by the Peloponnesians, yet the Lacedaemonians would have been abandoned, not willingly but of necessity, by their allies whose cities had been captured by the naval force of the Barbarian, and would have been left alone. And, being thus left alone, they would have shown forth great works and died nobly . . . So now, if someone said that *the Athenians were the saviors of Hellas*, he would have not have missed the truth (VII 139).

Epilogue

This, then, is Herodotus's historical truth: The Spartans would have "shown forth"—his standard term for deeds and doers that have flared into prominence or deserve to—great deeds. They would have died nobly and memorably in defeat, as they did at Thermopolae, had not the Athenians once more stood staunchly with Hellas and lived to save her, as they had done at Marathon. Had they, by Themistocles' agency, not managed their resistance with such effective cunning, I think that Herodotus, consequently a Persian subject, could not have written his work at all or would have produced merely a collection of memorable exploits.

The Athens, however, of which his *History* tells, was for him not just a wonderful place; it was "historical" in our, latter-day sense—destiny-laden with freedom and equality, somewhat as Toqueville, in the Introduction to *Democracy in America*, presents America's democratic equality as a "providential fact." To be sure, when Herodotus was composing his *History* some half a century later, Athens was, so he intimates, by her own overreaching, aborting her own destiny.

Thus Herodotus's invention, an inquiry that is temporally deep and spatially cosmopolitan, takes on its third sense, besides those of a *memorial of wondrous works* and of an *account of the place where a great and complex idea eventuated*—freedom (*eleutheria*) confirmed by civic participation (*isagoria*): *prophecy, the foreshadowing of a calamity* that will soon cause Athens "to be history" (in our colloquialism).

Herodotus would have died a happier man than he did, I imagine, ending up as an emigrant to Italian Thurii,[79] had he known that the Athens where he composed his work, was, after all, the future, realized in the Barbarians of the West, the Americans—and not least because of his *History*. He would have thought himself the most fortunate of historians in having an epoch to

---

79. Thurii was an Athenian Panhellenic colony, so perhaps after all, just the right venue for him to sit out the Peloponnesian War.

show forth during which, in Aristotle's terms, "what *has* come to be" is also "what *might* come to be"—a "historical" moment when the "might" of historical futurality and the "might" of philosophical possibility coincided, when *history and poetry were at one.*[80]

Addendum

The encircling schema differs from one proposed by François Hartog in *The Mirror of Herodotus: The Representation of the Other in the Writing of History* (1980, trans. by Janet Lloyd, Berkeley: University of California Press, 1988). Hartog addresses, with cautious indefiniteness, the question concerning the relation of the two Herodotuses (p. 371), one being the ethnographer of the Barbarians (first half of the *History*), the other being the historian of the Persian Wars (second half). It is a version of the question whether the work has unity. I hope to have shown that the Barbarian ethnography is definitely integral to the crux of Herodotus's *History*, which is the delineation of Greek freedom, civic and personal.

Hartog, furthermore, draws attention to several Herodotean schemata (my term), such as geographic anti-symmetries and ethnographic inverses. So far, so good. However, he presents Herodotus's "rhetoric of otherness" as implicitly guided by a "rule of the excluded middle" (pp. 258–259): Herodotus, unable to cope with three-way oppositions (as Hartog thinks), tends to reduce ethnic antitheses to dualities. For example, in comparing the fighting ways of Greeks, Persians, and Scythians, he soon turns Persians into "Greeks" by

---

80. Aristotle, recall, says that "poetry is more philosophical and more serious than history" (*Poetics* 1451 6).

attributing to them Greek strategies, so as to obtain a simpler opposition. These assimilations do indeed occur, but if all the *basic* oppositions were to be thought of as, so to speak, radial, connecting the one Greek center in turn to each member of the Barbarian periphery, then the "excluded middle" device would be merely occasional, while the primary antithesis would be (as I think) between the unique Greeks and each of the multiple others, every pair contributing to the definition of Hellenicity in terms of a different foil.

Imaginative Conservatism

I wish to dedicate this essay to a writer of books whose greatness is at once utterly at home in America and quite without spatio-temporal boundaries, Marilynne Robinson, who produces in reality the images I only analyze, and thereby not only saves but augments the tradition I love— the aboriginal imaginative conservative, one who celebrates the glory of the commonplace.

When Winston Elliott invited me to become a Senior Contributor to *The Imaginative Conservative* I had misgivings. "Is this an honor honestly come by?" I asked myself. Am I a conservative, true blue and staunch? A conservative at all? Would a political conservative have twice voted for our current president, and for my reasons? Because he could speak both in the faith-borne periods of a black preacher and the consideringly correct paragraphs of a Harvard professor. Because he was physically graceful and young. (My disapproving conservative friends claim I fell in love with his ears—and I had no deniability.) Because he was half-black (a way of putting it that suppresses, absurdly, that he is half-white) and I felt this to be great cause for national pride. But, then again, I thought he was a pragmatic crypto-conservative (in which I turned out to be half-wrong, though all too right if you ask his Left). And because nothing has more eroded my political conservatism than the mulish obstructionism he's met with from the Far Right, that miserable simulacrum of Conservatism.[1]

Yet, "imaginative conservative" does just about describe me. If Winston will forgive my boasting: he tells me that the title of his site is borrowed from some writing of mine of long ago. So I'm entitled, somehow. Let me then put "political" conservatism aside for a—long—moment. Later I'll want to show why an "imaginative" conservative might be all over the political map, as occasion arises: right, center, left—reactionary (disgustedly oppositional), moderate (prudently dithering), and radical (exuberantly reformist).

So, as always in life, having found the phrase that wins my adherence, it's time to figure out what it means. What's "imaginative"? What's "conservative"? And how does the adjective modify the noun and the noun support its adjective? For my basic assumption is that—let other persuasions appeal to bleeding hearts, Christian conscience, or political realism—a conservative should have, first of all, recourse to self-awareness, mindfulness, *reflection*. One last confession before I get to it: none of the subjoined lucubrations are anything but second editions, so to speak, recollections and rephrasings of thoughts thought and re-thought over the decades. But perhaps that is in itself a sort of conservatism—to allow one's convictions to modify and self-reform, but not to be given to swoops and loops and U-turns.

First: Temperamental Disposition

Candor seems to require the admission that conservatism is a *temperamental disposition*.[2] This concession explains a fact that would otherwise leave us nonplussed: that all people aren't conservatives. Conservatism is, I think, a disposition to delight in repetition, reference, resonance, recollection—to feel at home with twice-told tales. The other temperament relishes what is novel, decodable, anechoic, contractile.

All the nominal terms of the "conservative set" (not, God help us, a "mind-set," as if the intellect were green aspic-in-a-mold) imply the experience of twiceness, of iteration. "This event has happened before, takes it meaning from elsewhere, reverberates with bygone music, recalls its memory from beyond." A term borrowed from theology helps: This imaginative experience is the human counterpart of the divine *nunc stans*. As "standing now" encompasses all the phases of time—past, present, and future—in one eternal present, so the imagination collapses all times into one, phase-fraught Now. As Socrates thinks that "the unexamined life is not lived," meaning that nothing has properly happened until it has been tethered in reflection, so the imaginative conservative feels that the unimagined life has not eventuated, that nothing has come to pass until it has been reiterated, rehearsed in the conservatory of the IMAGINATION.

The antithetical set of adjectives can be comprehended under a phase-term from history: modernity,
from *modo*, "just now." To be modern means to eschew
a time-fraught—in favor of a time-divorced—Now, to
be as temporally abrupt, to achieve as pure a punctual-
ity as possible. For the narrower the now, the speedier
the temporal progress. Thus modernity is tied to novelty; "novel" is what has never existed before and will
not last long after. Novelty requires innovation, newness
for its own sake. In matters human, recent modernity
seeks "decodable" complexes, meaning experiences that
can be represented as encryptions of discrete rational elements. It prefers "anechoic," echoless, modes, the flat
factuality of informational data. Finally, I term it "contractile," because it tends to superseding rather than
absorbing, to displacing rather than accommodating us-
ages. In sum, our modernity is fast and fleeting.

I've written in abstractions here. Modernity is just a
summary term and has no power whatsoever, and the
set of attributes I've picked out is neither complete nor
really generic. Moreover, I can't believe that the two dis-
positions I'm attempting to delineate aren't both latent
in all of us, and that the one I adhere to can't be elicited in us all by imaginative education. It's just that in
order to clarify imaginative conservatism, I needed a
sort of antithetical bogeyman. Nonetheless, with that
caveat declared, I don't want to recant my claim that
people do, by and large, fall into various positions along
this temperament-spectrum and that its right and left
can be summed up, somewhat more insouciantly, like
this: Imaginative conservatives mess around pragmati-

cally *sub specie aeternitatis* (under the aspect of eternity) while the other side wants righteously to rectify the world right now. I think good things get done somewhere in the middle of this spectrum. But now I've veered off into political action, when I've made it my brief to talk about the soul. Well, what politics is to public life, education is to the soul. So shifting to the second part of this analogy, let me say prospectively that nothing—*nothing*—seems to me as important to our communal life as the discriminating provision of children's imagination. More of that at the end.

Second: Reflection

With this twice-lived, iterative mode of the soul goes a way of thinking that I've already named—*reflection*. Here's what it means to me: a receptive readiness, an intentional openness. "Intentional" is a medieval term for the way the mind tends toward, reaches for, the world. There are many kinds of mentation, such as calculational, which converts qualities into quantities (as in "It's hot because the thermometer is up to 95°"); analytic, which breaks the world up into its components (as in "Here's a revolution, let's take it apart into its religious, historical, political, economic, etc., factors"); methodical, which applies a tried-and-true procedure to situations (as in "Here's a patient, let's get his insurance, emergency number, vital signs, etc."); symbolic, which turns beings into labels (as in "Here's a school in trouble, let's do some re-branding and achieve name-recognition").

All these ways have their profitable efficiencies as well as their loss-producing dysfunctions. One had better be good at them—but as a *user*, not as a true *believer*. They don't intend to construe the world; they mean to construct it. Not so reflection. It is a figure for attentional receptivity: send the beam of your interest out to things and receive the light returned by your object. (Language for the soul's activity is perforce figurative.) There is a strong assumption here to be sure, a realism: the world that confronts us contains—be it at a first or second remove—substances, given natures that are somehow accessible to us. (This "somehow" covers shelves of philosophical technicalities.) "Reflection" honors this givenness. It expresses the priority of being over making, of receiving over manipulating, of nature over second nature. Other modes conceptualize; they produce concepts, thought-constructs, mental schematisms, "large-mannered motions" intended to have great generality, that is, *ideologies*. Reflection brings back basic notions of beings, thoughts that have great *specificity* in the sense of being replete with the nature of things, that is, *ideas*. *Species*, recall, is Latin for the Greek philosophical term *idea* or *eidos*, that in things which is intelligible to us.

Is reflection, then, purely passive? Yes, insofar as openness is a kind of excitable passivity. In human terms, the reflective life implies that adherence, engagement, and commitment to the way things are, *love* in sum, are the inciting causes of thinking rather than, say, mere gawking curiosity or its equally unloving antithesis, pure practical utility.

Yet, to my mind the plans that spring from, and the actions that follow on, receptive thought ought to—indeed often do—jibe better with the world than those that are willfully inventive. One way to put it is this: Constructive thinking changes the world; receptive thought changes it for the better.[3] (Even the students of my own college, as good a lot as a teacher can hope for, are enough in the grip of modernity urgently to wish "to change the world," well before they have reflected much on how the world will look if they get their wish.) As so often, the trouble is terminal generality: abolish poverty, prejudice, inequality, etc., etc. Reflective thinking, given to according due respect to the way things are, tends to bring the "how" of execution much closer to the "what" of the desired outcome. This accretion of specificity, this involvement of means and ends, prevents some unintended consequences. Another way to put it is this: If your designs intend to save a cherished vision of the imagination, you will be more open to practical compromise, well knowing that the actualities of the soul are anyhow never fully realized in the world and that, moreover, getting your way completely is the prelude to perdition (a text for a sermon full of edifying anecdotes).

Third: Radicalism

The imaginative conservatism of such thinking is near neighbor to *radicalism*—not, I repeat *not*, extremism, which is a sort of secular fanaticism, aggressive all-out-ism, all-or-nothingism; nor even the inspid heterodoxy,

cluelessly advocated by educators, called "questioning"—
of situations, assumptions, elders. *Questioning* is secular inquisition, sneakily hostile inquiry. Its intention is to skewer the object and barbecue it. It is antithetical to *question-asking*, the central non-technique of reflection. A question affirms, at least as a starting point, the matter asked after. It imputes to its object the being that inquiry can wind itself around and the worth that arouses the interest implied in asking. The object of a question obliges by making of itself a sort of attractive nuisance, an irritating desire.

"Questioning," then, is reason in its suspiciously peering mode, and since its satisfactions are necessarily negative, it can never rest satisfied, except perhaps in the ultras of the mind, in mental excess. Horribly enough, the human beings who have talked themselves into these regions are met there by their fellows who've come by the short route—true believers in stark finalities. Here the far-out intellectuals and the hell-bent troops find each other; it's a human catastrophe in the making: Nazis, Soviets, in the last century.

Conservative radicalism means something quite different to me. Fanaticism is deliberate tunnel vision, chosen obliviousness of environments and surroundings, stark single-mindedness—the very opposite of the twice-lived imaginative life. The conservative is always in the middle of things, betwixt and between, *interestedly* engaged in the world's paradoxes and oppositions. Recall that "interest" (from the Latin *interesse*) means "to be among things," sufficiently composed not to fear compromise, moved enough to feel responsibility, whereas extremists are self-displaced to the far-out edges, where hot tempers and icy simplicities rule. (One of the marvels of Dante's hell is that Satan's Inferno is ice-cold.)

"Radical" means going to the roots. There is that eradicating radicalism I've described as extremism, which pulls growths up by the roots to exterminate them like weeds. But conservative radicalism digs deep in order to ground more securely by understanding more deeply the roots of the world. All the things we care about have, or so I think, a root to be understood, reflected on, replanted. (Thomas Aquinas, for example, speaks of *radix gratiae, habitus, peccati, virtutis, rationis*, "the root of grace, disposition, sin, virtue, reason.")

In such inspection the cankers also come to light. Thus every anchoring root of our country's political life turns out to have its attendant flaw, knowledge of which is a cause for shamed love. American patriotism is confirmed both in the resigned acknowledgment of our ineradicably inherent defects and in some participation in righting eradicable flaws. What other country's all-but national anthem can boast such a stanza:

America! America!
God mend thine every flaw,
Confirm thy soul in self-control,
Thy liberty in law!

Conservative radicalism is reflective rootedness.

Fourth: Philosophy

Now I must cast loose from this earth and go off into the wild blue yonder of *ontology*, an unjustly ogreish word, which means "the account of Being." Up until the middle of the last century, Being—what ultimately *is*—was the central interest of all philosophy in our Western tradition.

I want to claim that conservatives of the soul think *philosophically*—ipso facto. This claim goes somewhat against a very respectable conservative tradition that pits conservative moderation against philosophical extremism. It's a belief that deserves respect because it belongs to the tradition of traditionalism. I mean that this traditional belief values—as I do—what has slowly come to be, carries the past within, belongs to this specific place, cherishes the treasures delivered to us (*tradere*, "to deliver," "hand down") in two strands, sometimes from our imaginative and intellectual forbears (mine are Homer and Socrates), sometimes from our ethnic ancestors (mine are Joseph the Egyptianized Jew and David the kingly musician).

But the proponents of this beautiful dual tradition make what seems to me a big error. They mistake philosophy—the love of wisdom, the desire to know what's what, that opens itself receptively to beings—for ideology, the trading in thought-packages that willfully traffics in denuded rationalisms. They rightly value responsive reasonableness over manipulative rationality but forget that reasoning too can be a form of safekeeping.

Coercive rationality, moreover, plays only a very intermittent part in philosophy, which is—or so I think—given to all kinds of detail-invested thoughtfulness, particularly the imaginative kind. Read a really rationalist thinker, and you will find an occasionally smartly devised but mingy mythlet to illustrate a point. The reflective philosophers, on the other hand, allow their thought to clothe itself in grand myths—not so that we may luxuriate in our mortal version of what Wallace Stevens calls Jove's "mythy mind," fuzzy and static, but, on the contrary, to move our thinking about a multitude of matters: about the remarkable fact that we can receive non-spatial beings (divinities and fictions) into that psychic quasi-space called the imagination; about the mysterious nature of images themselves, that they both are and are not the beings they present; about our unexplained ability to extract intellectual truth from images, myths, parables, and those image-skeletons, diagrams; and, finally, about our astounding gift for thinking beyond the limitations of our language.

Far be it from me to demand that folks trying to live their lives should take on professional philosophy. Professors of philosophy belong to a guild like any other; they do what they were trained to do and what they are good at (to obfuscate or clarify as the state of the art may require) and what gains reputation and a livelihood. I am thinking of an unabashedly amateurish affair, everyone's business: to muse occasionally about the multifarious appearances that present themselves to our five external senses (why five?) and whether *ap-*

pearances are what there is or whether something supports them, something—that notorious *Being*—which they both hide and reveal; to meditate now and then on ourselves; to think about our thinking power, whether rationality is always or ever reasonable, whether rigorous reason is always right reason, whether thoughtfulness should be dead serious or actively playful, in short, to ask what is required to get responsibly from here to there in thinking; to wonder whether human beings have changed their nature over the millennia, whether something did change in human being when it turned, in early modernity, from being an embodied soul in God's world to being a disembodied subject constructing its own world (toward which inquiry a piece of learning is moderately helpful: at the dawn of our era, the word "subject," which had meant "the bearer of an object's qualities," flipped into "subjective consciousness," what we mean when we speak of our personhood, our subjectivity); and finally, to consider how we will be transformed if our bodies become mostly prosthetic artifacts and our souls withdraw largely into cyberspace.

Fifth: Divinity

It follows as the night the day that a conservative of any imagination will be concerned with *divinity*. Although there could be no obligation to be a believer in the conservatism I'm delineating, yet there might be a duty not to position oneself as a skeptic, meaning by "skeptic" a habitual questioner of the questioning type described above, someone who, under the mask of inquiry, intends corrosion.

The beginning is the disposition to feel respect, even awe, in the face of faith, to suppose that a faithful fellow human may, far from lacking critical ability, have been given a gift—called "grace" in theology. Next comes, or ought to come, a genuine (not an informational) desire to reflect on the possible reality of a root of all roots, to brew up some sympathy for the possibility of Scripture, meaning a book whose ultimate author is trans-human; to find the teachings of faith (dogma) and the contents of religion (ritual) engaging; and to be open to the grandeurs of theology and the wonder of the great doctors of divinity—that human beings of the most logically acute and humanly penetrating intelligence should be willing to turn the beginnings of their thought over to revelation and faith.

If belief does not eventuate (the best word in my vocabulary for its coming about), there is a reverent substitute, situated between belief and skepticism: good-faith agnosticism. "Agnosticism" literally means "not-knowing." Not knowing in good faith is, therefore, not making specious protestations of ignorance—a mask for spiritual indolence or crypto-skepticism. Despair strenuously developed, on the other hand, though possibly open to the charge of willfulness, also seems to me a good-faith position; so is serious atheism—a curious state of strenuous belief in a not-god, in God with a negative sign. In fact, the merely apparent openness of the agnostic who has adopted that position as a sort of effort-mitigation seems to me even more unbudgeable than that of the unbeliever who exists agitatedly fending off recapture by this non-existent God—such agonizing people live as serious figures in Dostoevsky novels, and in the world as well.

The agnosticism in which I have faith begins with a strong sense of human finitude—not others' but my own, a strong sense that I have no access to the bounds of my own existence, no credible news of that "undiscov'd country from whose bourn/No traveler returns." Thoughts of my essence, my "whatness," may well take me behind and beyond the here and now that characterizes my "thatness," my existence, but these existential, real life bounds are absolute. Well, perhaps not quite; after all, it is possible to imagine hell or paradise—indeed they are the imagination's prime subjects. So sometimes I feel a kind of shame at possibly waking up after death in a venue that is absolutely strange to me; the thought of being caught post-mortem in embarrassing ignorance invokes a sort of obligation to imagine possible afterlives. Oblivion, of course, is not a subject for the imagination, which is constitutionally incapable of hosting invisibility.

In sum, to think about a possible divine nature is an obligation not at all abrogated by divine inaccessibility. Here's another way to put it: The sense that I seriously don't know is not the end but the beginning; imagination can stand in for faith; thus the inquiry that saves our humanity is conserved. The ancient astronomers had a wonderful way of phrasing their task: "to save the appearances." They meant to find the mathematical hypotheses, the underpinnings, that would make the heavens intelligible. But it goes as well for the theological urge; its task is to thoughtfully save the hither world by hypotheses about the thither realm—and the imaginative conservative will want to participate.

Sixth: Populism

Now is the moment, when I've so run up the intellectual stakes, to say something of the *populism* that seems to me to fit the imaginative conservative.

The populism of the Right has, deservedly, a dubious reputation: no-nothing anti-intellectualism, anti-democratic demagoguery, exploitation of prejudice, hate-mongering. It's no better on the Left: dictatorships of the proletariat, leveling egalitarianisms, crowd-sourced pseudo-revolutions. The populism I mean is the political friendship on which, as Aristotle says, civic communities are founded. It is very American, and its Madisonian version seems to me particularly to suit the conservative temperament—democracy controlled by a constitution, mediated by representation, and diversified by the interest groups Madison calls factions. (I think of Madison as the most imaginative conservative statesmen I know of, imaginative in envisioning very specifically how things actually work on earth, conservative in devising an edgily innervating stability.)

The populism that seems to me to suit us is a friendly fellow-feeling based on sheer liking of our common public ways: the matter-of-fact courteous helpfulness of our casual encounters; the ready wit of our linguistic companionableness, the well-worn high jinks of our gestures; the commonsensical *unegalitarian* sense of *equal-*

ity, meaning the deep sense that *sub specie aeternitatis*, seen from the height of heaven, as it were, we are indeed all equal, of an equal creation but that, on the plateau of earth, we are quite unequally, or better, incommensurably, gifted; the consequent understanding that we are endowed from above with certain equal rights regarding our existence, but that seen on the shared level of earth we are all mysteries to each other and so, ipso facto, entitled to respect for our individual souls. It follows, I think, that you have to be very willful to enforce an egalitarianism of condition or of gifts on so incomparably diverse a lot as we are. (Examples for my own practical application: expect even an evidently warranted judgment of terminal stupidity passed on a fellow mortal to be someday nullified by unsuspected wisdom. Similarly for badness: expect even patent rogues to have some preserve of goodness in their souls. Despising is neither imaginative nor conservative.)

Similarly for cleverness. Contravening my own advice, I'm not a great respecter of pointy-headed intellectuals (a prejudice common to all sorts of conservatives). The first token of this type is Thersites in Homer's *Iliad* (whose head literally comes to a peak), a homely, narrow-shouldered, bandy-legged foot soldier among knights and a fellow of "measureless wordiness," who gets beaten up by Odysseus for his subversive social criticism. But—this is Homer's covert greatness—Thersites really is speaking truth to power; he's one of *us*.

I know perfectly well that these fellow-citizens, left and right, especially the latter, can be (unlike myself) pains in whatever part of the anatomy you prefer. They play deaf to reason, go on motoric rants, display fire-power (though mostly hunting rifles, the least scary of the whole worrisome miscellany) and all the other unamiable qualities for which the theoretical egalitar-ians and believers in "the people" of the Left tend to despise people. Still, for good sense, the middling major-ity (which is, lamentably, shrinking but still most of us) seems to me most trustworthy: decent, shrewd, often religious, not-so-simple, and—what is not to be under-rated—generally high on personal hygiene, and there-fore agreeable up close and personal. I'd rather see sovereignty with them (and so, with me) than with any other class I know. I've already mentioned the inequal-ities of personal excellence, of endowments, of which glories and dangers I, as a teacher, am acutely aware. True believers in creaturely equality ought to be, and, as I said, in this country often are, generously unegalitar-ian with respect to acknowledging gifts.

I can't claim really to have much of a feel for pop-ular culture, from wailing folksongs accompanied by plunky guitars to the succession of big-time musical en-tertainments of the last half-century. But a devotion to the works of traditional high culture just can't be a dis-qualifier for being a populist of the sort I've described—doesn't the most popular high of high culture, the Ninth, claim that in joy all men will be brothers?—popu-lism, albeit expressed in politically incorrect, gendered language.

A last thought under this rubric: I have a notion that the whole country would be a bit better if our language were a little more taut, a little more succinct. Not only would shy people be more apt to get a word in, but the linguistic law of diminishing returns would be properly observed—the longer you talk, the less anyone hears. (Case in point: modern tyrants compel crowds to listen to six-hour rants.) The Gettysburg Address took just over two minutes to deliver. I think we would all like each other a little better if we had the occasional common experience of the brief grandeur of a Lincoln-like speech. Am I dreaming?

Seventh: Time

That brings to mind *time*, surely the concern of an imaginative conservative, who lives now in, now out of time, who sometimes thinks and, in stretches, reasons collectedly and again muses and meditates vagrantly. (Buddhist-oriented readers must forgive me for this hijacking of their central practice; in the Western tradition, for instance in Descartes, "meditation" refers to imaginative thinking. For my part, I experience vagrant mentation often but can form no conception—such is my residual respect for rationality—of a mind perfectly cleared of all thinking, in the Eastern mode.)

So here is this particular conservative's take on time: I think he, or—as I, a woman, may say without having political correctness imputed to me—she, will have a bias *against the future*. It sounds very like profanity to say so in an age in which almost all time is fugitive *but* the future. It is, however, this very bully-future I'm against. "X is coming, like it or not"; "You can't stop Y [usually putative progress], so go with it"; "We have to change or we'll be left behind." These are threats, even "existential" threats, as they say.

Well, surely I don't have to submit to what I don't like, surely I can go against rather than with "it," surely I can opt to be left behind, if that's where I want to be. After all, it's well known that if you fall behind for a long enough time, you'll end up way ahead: "The first shall be last and the last first." The future is not what's inevitably coming but what *you* are *willing* to have others call up for you and what *you* are *ready* to summon a slightly hysterical welcome for. You could opt out, live around it. "To hell with you" is an apt profanity, when used toward time-bullies, for they are emissaries from the realm of No Exit, which *is* hell.

Here's a truth, an ontological one, meaning one concerning the way things are. (Below I'll reiterate that a true conservative is an ontologist, an account-giver of Being.) There *is* no future. It is not a region, and so nothing can come to or at us from there. There *are* hopes, expectations, and plans. They are *now.* "He will come to dinner" means I expect him and he plans to come, not that this future dinner guest, who is still taking a shower at home, is somehow already marching toward my house.

There are, as far as I can tell, two futures right now. One is fixed and determined by the laws of nature plus present conditions. Since no living soul is in full possession of all the conditioning facts, no one knows what will happen of necessity, even if he is convinced that the future is fixed. On the whole, forecasts are pretty reliable nowadays, so it makes sense, for example, to invest in real estate, as if the Eastern coastline (the one I care about) might be partly underwater in 2030. So it will probably be—unless . . .

The other future is fairly completely up to us. For instance, if we wish our young more or less to disappear into electronic virtuality, that's entirely up to us. "Us" is a tricky word here; it means both you and me, and we may wish for different futures. So what's coming is not entirely in my power or in yours, but it is most assuredly not in the power of that utter non-being, *the* Future.

I might inject here that the bully-futurist is not the only bully I need to stand up to. The bully-conservative, my disreputable cousin, is equally unlovable. I mean that incarnation of one-eyed againstness, of dug-in recalcitrance, of pseudo-rational reaction, that has brought Congress into disrepute (from which it will recover when the people's good sense again prevails over their urgent fears, as it always does). Therefore, complementary to resisting surrender to the specious siren-song of an inevitable future is withstanding the noisy rant of fear-inspired reaction.

If the Future is rightly exposed as self-fulfilling prophecy, as willfulness disguised as prescience, what about the past? The past seems like the proper province, the homeland, of the conservative soul. It has, however, one small defect: If the future is *not yet*, the past is *no more*. The past has passed away; it's dead and gone. It's nowhere on earth to be found.

I should know. I used to be an archaeologist. We regarded the artifacts and bones we (very methodically) dug up after 2,700 years of resting in peace, as testimonials of the past—no, as pieces of the past. But that was one of the axiomatic illusions all professions require to keep working. My pot-sherds weren't past. They were present, now-existing. And their age was *our* attribution and their meaning *our* interpretation. A perfectly innocent intelligence would not have discerned any pastness in those precious snippets of civilization sitting in the soil along with dumbly timeless pebbles.

And yet—the past has a smidgin *more thereness* than the future, which is why the sedate conservative has a tad more solidity than the labile progressive. Where then is the past, if not on earth? *In memory.* The past exists because we remember. The soul is a lamination of time-signed memories and projections. (The language is mine, but the thought comes from Augustine, the most time-wise philosopher-theologian I know of.)

Some of these memories arise from personal experience, some from outside transmissions. Some are corroborable and falsifiable, some are beyond the pale of evidence. The memorial past is all the past there is. If it has more thereness, more existence, than the future, it is because the projections that *are* the future are, after all, just modified cullings of memory. The future—our particular future—is mostly past-plus-technology, that is, memory-images plus special effects—confidently expectant science fiction.

So what's left to life? The Now. And when is that? When asked what time it was, my favorite philosopher, Yogi Berra, answered, "You mean now?"—a counter-question that has no possible answer. It's always and never now. The Now, when analyzed, is a point without parts, to save us from which the psychologists have proposed a "specious present," the moment of actual consciousness. It can be extended to the span of immediately active memory (at least for the young; for the old what happened three hours before has gone into deeper oblivion than what happened three score years ago).

If our analogue watches, instead of ticking and skipping along in increments, were as truly continuous as are the starry heavens they model (which Plato called "the moving image of eternity," eternity being the *nunc stans* mentioned above), no Now would be distinguishable from any other; they would all meld into each other. So it is a genuine mystery how we manage to exist—a source of irritated rationalization to the problem-solvers and of acceptant awe to the reverence-minded. (*Nota bene*. In fact I rejoice in problem-solving, from household malfunctions to human embroilments to political perplexities. But I think of it as a lesser human mode than contemplation.) There is a famous saying by Marx here adapted by me: "Philosophy has hitherto aimed to *understand Being*; it is time for it to *solve problems*."[4] That, I would claim, is pure perversity. And the opposite is pure conservatism: first apprehend Being, then get to doing. More of that below.

Thus the time-phase of which there is, so to speak, the most, is the past, and this past is lodged in personal but also in *public* memory. There resides the tradition that is the conservative domain, almost by definition, for the handing down (once again, *tradere*, Latin for "transmitting," "handing on") of past treasure is, after all, any conserver's prime business. Conservatives are ipso facto conservers, conservators. Moreover, the conserving absorption of public into personal memory well describes the process of education. Put otherwise, education is in part the enlivening activity whereby the lifeless letter of external memory is revivified in the interior soul under the tutelage of someone in whom the tradition has already come to life. At least that is education for children: the stocking, the provisioning, of the imaginative memory with the goods of the tradition or tradition-to-be. (In current cognitive-science terms this accumulation of memorial treasure is prosaically called "storage.") For older students, the other part of education also comes into play, the incitement of reflection, of appreciative and, on occasion, condemnatory critique. For, contrary to the current judgment against "judgmentalism," judgment is what we were put on the earth to exercise—though not driven by pedagogic needling, but by exigent attention.

So the reappropriation of the sculpture carved, the book written, the music composed long ago, is the business of cultivating education. The original meaning of cultivation is the loosening of soil and the killing of weeds to allow plants to grow—so education as cultivation is a really good metaphor gone disastrously dead. It might sound as if education in the conservative understanding had to do with the past that has passed away and its zombie-like re-animation. But the real past, the past of memory, is precisely un-passed; it lives after all in the soul, and the soul is vitality itself. That is why conservatism is averse to "historicism," the notion that the chronological time you live in makes you what you are, with the consequence that when your time is up, you're history, dead and gone, mummy for scholars. (There is an academic mafia, contract killers who produce rigid time-corpses out of the past and then position and re-position them; this exercise is called revisionism.) That is also why, from historically meticulous restoration to insouciantly inventive historical theme parks, the smell of dry death, of Miss Havisham's cobwebbed stasis, hangs over the reanimation business, no matter that its venues are spider-free and squeaky-clean. These well-researched tableaus are the opposite of true renaissance, of rebirth, the present reappropriation of the past. The tradition rightly taken in is, I think, a *privately* performed renaissance, a revivification of the stock delivered to the soul's storehouse.

The twice-lived life, the iterated existence I spoke of above, is memory-bound, for nothing has really happened until it locks into its proper past, finds its background myth. Memory provides the backdrop that sets the scene for the event—here and now. Perhaps some sort of temperament can live in the unresonant, referenceless, anechoic Now—but I can't imagine that experience.

To recapitulate, and more radically: The past that is alive and present, the memorial past, the ongoing renaissance of the soul, abolishes in its very conserving potency the distancing properties of chronological time and material space. Why should spatial distance and remote time be principles of separation when their inhabitants all together dwell in the soul's memory? *Nihil humanum alienum mihi* ("nothing human is alien to me"), if I have a conserving memory and a memorial imagination.

We are lucky in our Western heritage, lucky that it is a *great* tradition that has been bequeathed to us, and lucky that so much has been enough valued to escape the degradation of passing time. But here is a question: Is it the antiquity that a conservative actually tends to value in this tradition, more than its contents? I have a little Attic cup dating from the fifth century B.C.E. sitting beside me. It holds paper clips, but every once in a while I "come to" and a frisson runs down my spine as I think, "2,450 years back and perhaps a little Athenian kid was drinking his milk from this." Mere antiquity has its peculiar charms to which the dispositional conservative is perhaps particularly sensitive. But all in all the glory of the tradition—a tradition primarily in books—as I've tried to lay it out, is not in its pastness but in its presence. These books speak directly and rousingly to me and my friends, known and unknown; moreover, they are in dialogue with each other, on either side of their temporal position. To their predecessors they respond by acceptance and/or rejection; to their successors they attempt to project their influence. And as its individual speakers have greatness, so their conversation has grandeur. Raphael in the "School of Athens" was right to put them all in one venue as contemporaries. Imaginative conservatism is not *essentially* time-involved.

One last temporal consideration: What is the conservative disposition toward the New, that I seem to have proscribed above? Newness may appear in two modes. There is "new to me"—all the things I never knew. "All human beings," I think with Aristotle, "are hungry to know." So we're all avid for knowledge already known to others. But sometimes there is also "new in the world." Some of this newsy news is old stuff, re-costumed. But there *are* things truly new and new in themselves: new phenomena and new knowledge—not novelties, newly invented for the sake of newness, but newly discovered because the realm of nature or of the intellect was willing to yield to the importunities of ingeniously avid research. I've studied some science and some mathematics—and even some philosophy—that boggles the mind in its never-before-heard-of newness and its revolutionary re-formation of human and natural being—that gives the lie to the Preacher who claims that "there is nothing new under the sun." I won't list examples because I'm averse to name-dropping, but every reader will have a supply. To my mind, the proper conservative response to true newness (as opposed to hyped-up novelty) is to assimilate it as best we can, to integrate it into the dialectic of the tradition, where it settles into its place—and in ceasing to be so discom-bobulating, becomes really interesting.

Eighth: Politics

Here is an excursus on *politics*, for surely being an imaginative conservative, that is, primarily a conservative of the soul, must have some proper public consequences, articulable in a sort of political credo. Here's mine: fairly reliable reasonableness in matters of policy and utter unpredictability in party adherence. I'd be sorry to think anyone *could* predict my vote, or that they *couldn't* count on my having communicable reasons.

Yet there are probably also ingrained predispositions: to incrementalism not closed to sudden dramatic intervention; to retreat-ready-positions on policy with—a very few—unbudgeable principles; to being generally in the mainstream with occasional last-ditch-loner holdouts. Back at Yale, more than three score years ago I learned one thing from my numismatics professor (not much about those beastly little coins of which numismatics is the study). He was department chairman and told me his manner of governance, "Pure principles and corrupt administration." He meant: *Never* do what's plain wrong but compromise yourself shamelessly on all the confused issues—that would, thirty years later, bedevil my life as a dean. (A note on "plain wrong": It goes without saying that any judgment of wrong—or right— is *mine*, but that doesn't imply "wrong *for me*," as relativists claim. Moral judgment is, I think, in its very nature universal; otherwise it is mere preference, morally weightless. If that isn't a conservative opinion these days, I wouldn't know what is.)

So in sum, protectiveness of what is of slow growth and has endured—has both suffered and lasted through times and places. And as a complement, sudden action when the time has come—readiness to join, never the revolt of the masses, but the revolution of citizens, whose best model is our own American revolution.

And always that insistence that big-hearted generalities be costed out in practical specificities, for sentimentally expansive mantras tend to issue in restrictively rational prescriptions. Further, even (or especially) in politics, there's a temperamental preference for what has a human face and a distinctive flavor over what is standardized and sanitized, for what is free rather than planned, natural rather than plastic, small rather than large—in short, for the whole litany of a conservationist sensibility, provided that enthusiasm for its realization doesn't overwhelm care for people's present livelihoods. (Again, an example to represent concretely the whole dispositional complex: a preference for the analogue over the digital, for what is spatial, shapely, figurative, patent, over what is linear, cypher- and fact-like, encrypted. But perhaps I am sliding into personal taste rather than true-to-type delineation.)

Ninth: Materialism

There was a philosophy professor whose lectures I sat in on for a while at Yale (incidentally, the only real academic philosophy class I ever attended; therein was my salvation: the ignorance of academic philosophy permits the bliss of occasional insight). He used to say, when making a mental leap, "By a natural and easy transition, we now come to . . . ," so I now come to stuff and its ism, *materialism*.

Political conservatives do associate themselves with physical and notional accumulations—commodities and capital, profits and power. That's fine by me, as they said in my childhood Brooklyn. I'm not in love with stuff, per se; I have a rule for my little house: one thing in, one thing out; it doesn't apply to books. But I do hang on to, even love, some *things*, for example, that little Attic cup I mentioned above. To me, an imaginative conservative doesn't trash things but accords them a limited respect as being incarnations of human effort. Nor does he invest in objects designed for obsolescence—a euphemism for trashing. But this strain of disapproval is an old song and sometimes tiresome. So by and large, I think people should do with their money what they like and throw away (into the designated bins, if you please) what they want to be rid of. In fact, I would wish people to have what they want, and if they want stuff, on their head be it. Gorging isn't elegant, but it's human; conspicuous consumption isn't refined, but it's very human. People don't have to like what I like, particularly since the world is surely full of potential friends and sufficiently stocked with actual ones, who do like what I like.

All of which is to say that, given a choice between the disgusting materialism of the American middle and the sanctimonious spirituality of the elite, I'll take disgusting materialism. To the bottom of my heart, I'm what my students would call a freak—a First Amendment freak: freedom (within the law) first, and goods, even refined ones, will eventuate. Indeed here's a case for pretty radical conservatism: Let everyone talk as they like, and pray people won't take advantage; they're more likely to stay civil if not inhibited by rules of correctness.

I would go so far as to say that I find offense-taking somewhat offensive. This is the real world, live with it. So what if some oaf subjects me to anti-Semitism? Let's *not* make a federal case of it. I want the law to protect my person from harm, not my soul from insult. Confirm thy *soul* in *self-control*, thy *liberty* in *law*.

That was a bit of a digression from materialism. But this next point about immaterialism *is* the point. I have a real fear of virtuality; it makes me appreciate good old-fashioned thing-devotion. I think the diminution of the spacious imagination and the oblivion of the time-honored tradition that seem to be the unavoidable consequences of being glued to a dinky little tablet, reduced to twittering language, dispersed all over space, addicted to instantaneousness, tethered by connectivity, together with all sorts of illusions about wisdom accruing from infinite information, and the blessings of foreshortened time, are humanly deleterious and the prelude to a psychic implosion.

There was an obnoxious wisdom late in the last century—obnoxious since it was of the "like it or not" kind—that "the medium is the message." It was catchy hyperbole in any case. The medium merely abrades the substance, but that moderated version *has* come true: the content reflects the format, and the media format is not substance-friendly. Yet, as always, the people who know how to confine the medium to a means can do wonderful things with it. But that takes reflection—self-searching and self-control.

I think that the psychic implosion in store for an addicted generation will be awful, more so when the confident prophecy of a total-immersion virtual world, generated from within the brain, begins to be realized. Imaginative conservatives should prepare to resist, though they probably can't expect to have their political operatives with them in this battle.

My half-shelf of books on the digital age is full of references to "virtual reality." "Virtual" *means* "inactual," for God's sake.

Tenth: Soul

It's necessary to talk once more about the soul. It is a currently proscribed term; mind or consciousness are allowed. Their contexts are utterly different. I'll pick just one aspect. The soul is traditionally regarded as embodied, though separable in thought and perhaps in death; contemporary mind or consciousness is either an emergent aspect of the brain or simply identical with it. It would take pages to explicate this, so let me stick with "soul" because, since I'm not a brain scientist, I have no obligation to be a reductionist. An interim compromise with those who deny that they have a soul would be: You do without it and give me mine. Since some of the soul-deniers are relativists; they, at least, shouldn't balk at this solution. The reason the soul comes up again is because the novel world of the previous paragraph was technology-based, which leads to a scary division between cluelessly dexterous users and technique-savvy insiders—parasitical profiteers and controlling operators. That makes me ask, "What are imaginatively conservative *modes of thought*?" They can't be either of the above.

Far above, I said I would argue the claim that conservatives should be philosophical—nay, more: interested in the deepest delving into Being and its account, ontology.

Conservatives, in the tradition of their English fore-runners, tend to be suspicious of rationalism in human governance, of the impositions of righteous reason, and rightly so. They know the dark undersides of bright ideas. But insofar as this aversion makes them anti-philosoph-ical and causes them to forego theory for practicality, it rests, as I said, on a misapprehension. Philosophy is rational only in stretches and rationalistic never. Some-times thinking things out requires rigorous episodes of correct reasoning; it cannot, as the love of wisdom, ever mean shoe-horning the way things are into logi-cistic preconceptions—and that is what it means to be rationalistic.

I think there *are* modes of mindfulness that should appeal to a conservative, especially an imaginative one. I use the prescriptive "should" because when all is said and done the notion that a conservative could afford not to think his way as far into the depths as possible is just absurd. What is his tradition but a mutually responsive series of attempts to touch bottom or take the heights? "We've always done it that way" or "That just isn't done" are humanly considerable arguments, but they work for settled custom, not for our ever-inchoate tra-dition as I understand it—they're conservative but not so imaginative.

Here, then, are some non-rationalistic mental modes relevant to imaginative conservatism. First, conservative *imaginativeness*. All memorable philosophy—this is not the last time I'll say it—has recourse to images, some re-splendently panoramic, some denudedly diagrammatic. Images provide both the levering devices of thinking on its way and the embracing completion beyond reason's reach. Philosophy also relies on analogical insights, which are the chief works of philosophical imagination; in fact, analogy is to thinking what metaphor is to poetry. Both render manifest the same structure in different domains; both are imaginatively coherence-producing without rationalistically forcing identity.

Second, conservative *thinking*. It is almost a redundancy. Even mordant, skewering critique or refutation is destructive only as a finality; as a prelude to positive inquiry, it just clears the approaches to an object of desire. Inquiry itself, question-asking, is carefully conservative of its aim; a bona fide question is a premonitory intimation that cautiously seeks its substance, an anticipatory outline that tentatively lays itself about its object. It is the opposite of murdering to dissect.

Given these two mental modes, imagining and thinking, here are, further, two philosophical approaches that a conservative might welcome. I call them *hierarchy* and *comprehension*; they are complementary.

A "hierarchy" is a sacred rank-order. It seems to be an indwelling urge in human beings' thinking to assign gradations of worth, of superiority and inferiority. As a conservative I'm not so much for designations of inferiority, especially when it comes to human beings—and their diverse powers, which tend to be respected inversely to their functional scope. (Example: In traditional philosophical gradations of human capacities, that very imagination I so esteem tends to rank low—even though it is pervasively employed.) But, to be sure, where excellence or greatness is marked out, mediocrity and smallness are apparently implied. In hierarchical judgment, however, there is gradation, yet every member of the sacred order is, ipso facto, dignified. Another way to put this, one particularly relevant to humanity is this: In many respects, both natural and conventional, we are certainly rankable and so, unequal, but by this very fact of our common humanity, we are also at once equal and essentially of the same degree. And, yet beyond, insofar as this essence expresses itself of necessity in individual accidents, we are actually incommensurable, not subject to a common measure. It seems to me a conserving—and an imaginative—way to see the world: dignifying hierarchy.

As hierarchy pertains to gradation, so comprehension concerns inclusion. Meditations on life and world will, I think, inevitably dwell on what's in and what's out. I mean what is estimably thinkable and what is beyond the pale. Perhaps the primary, the ultimate, example, is Being and Non-being: what can manifest itself in existence, in specific "thisness" and its respectabilities, as against what has no underlying substance or apparent qualities, what is pure denial, perfect devoidness, total negation. For believing Christians, the representatives of these oppositions are respectively the Creator and Satan, the Adversary; for philosophical pagans (among which I rank myself), Being and Non-being are, as I said, the ultimate categories. Of these, Being has my cordial sympathy, Non-being my fascinated respect.

"Comprehension," as I intend it, is the mode of thinking that finds a way after all to include both members of the opposition, the In and the Out, in a whole.

One way to inclusiveness is to consider that the confines of what I positively approve are equally the limits of its negative complement: the latter therefore cooperates in the definition of the former and is thus a necessary aspect of all positive being. A related way is to consent to live with enough duplicity (in the literal sense, enough ambivalence) to accept even the devil's going to and fro in the world because his presence puts the whole Creation on alert, just as Non-being, when conceived as scattered through Being, invigorates it by diversifying it: every *this* shapes up by being *not that*. The greatest piece of ontology known to me, Plato's *Sophist*, achieves this triumph of philosophical cunning by interpreting all-pervasive Non-being as Otherness, Diverseness, the ontological ground of that very inclusive human diversity which is a current American preoccupation: every not-Me is an Other, necessary to the deep constitution of the world.

Political conservatives are not famous for tolerance. So much the more ought they, in their proper thoughtful mode, to gain a reputation for an inclusiveness more deeply grounded than in the unreliable vagaries of mere putting up with each other, called "tolerance." I'm suggesting that a notion such as "comprehension" might serve.

One more, last, conservative approach that comes to my mind (surely there are others) starts from the second most fundamental question of ontology, that of *universal-and-particular.* Earlier I referred to the unique incommensurability of individuals, which ultimately puts them beyond the common measure that gauges equality and inequality. Yet, I intimated, we could not be individuals were we not instances of a genus, tokens of a type, particulars of a universal—be it "rational animal" or, as an ancient wag said, "featherless biped," or the highest creation, or "person," or some more recent conceptual construct.

But always the question is: What are we *more*, the representative of a kind or an ultimately unique individual? The question becomes politically charged when our highest belonging is reassigned, as it is in "identity politics," from a common humanity to a religious, racial, ethnic, or gendered essence. Note that I have written a conservative prejudgment into the phrasing of the problem, namely that our essence is being human and the other categories come afterwards in importance, or are perhaps even just contingent constructs—intellectual underpinnings devised intentionally to support struggles for special acknowledgment and for power-bestowing rights.

That's my first sense of this future-fraught matter, but my considered belief is that it is incumbent on conservatives to think it out on the most fundamental level: how true essences, the basic natures that are universally attributed to a group, are to be determined, and how they are preserved and modified—"specified"—in individuals. We cannot respect, preserve, save, or conserve, that to which we have not extended the regard of our thoughtful consideration. Well, to be sure, we can, but we will do it ham-fistedly (or as the British so pungently say, "cack-handedly").

To me it seems an assignment that a conservative must not only accept along with everyone else, but is particularly well constituted to carry off, for conservative thinking traditionally prides itself on its concreteness, and that is what's wanted here, at least to begin with. Look at this concretely particular being and try to see him or her (of course I'm thinking of someone I know) now as a concretely particular realization of an assembly of categories, say, female, African-American, working woman, praise-singer, AME member[5]—and then again as a human being, essentially a walking universal and only accidentally an instance. Is there a right order for my listing of categories? How is the order manifested in the concrete being? What must I take in, what look past, to do the actual person justice? What wonderful (no, wondrous) melding of complexion and character make for concretely human, *not* abstractly ideological, respect and affection? I call this *episode* of attentive thinking "applied ontology." (Of course, I don't go around doing it all the time—in fact too rarely.) You can call it what you like—though perhaps better not "psychology." 'Tis a consummation devoutly to be wished that more of us fairly right-minded people would try to be frequently mindful as well.

Eleventh: Imagination

In my penultimate consideration, I come to the term closest to my heart—*imaginative*, for me the dominant term in this phrase "imaginative conservative"; I'm a conservative primarily because this adjective, I'll claim, correctly modifies its noun, though the converse also has its force: imaginativeness tends towards conservatism. For example, imagination gives political ideas their concreteness and forestalls, to some degree, unintended consequences. You have a cure-all program: tell me in concretely imagined detail how it will work out in real life, and also where you may get exactly what you don't want. *That* takes imagination of the literal sort I'm about to lay out. I was talking to a sympathetic friend about this essay and by way of keeping me from one-sidedness, he said, "But the others [liberals, he meant] also have imagination." "For instance?" I said. "Well, they envision a better world, a world free of . . . [a litany of ills]" We both began to laugh, because neither of us could see a thing—neither anyone's real land (there being some three-hundred-plus countries, as I recall), nor any specific desire (there being an infinity of those), nor any concrete plan (with escape routes). These goodhearted wishings were not imaginations but ideations, resulting in "ideas," bright ones. Once, long ago, "idea" did indeed connote ultimate repleteness; now it mostly means a mental fixation on a gift-wrapped thought-package.

At this near-last moment, I ought to define the *conservatism* whose imaginativeness I have wanted to analyze. Definition is dictionary business, and I often have recourse to Partridge's *Origins* (an etymological dictionary), in part because he's not overscrupulous about morphological fact, but very attached to what words mean or meant to their speakers. So: *con-* is an intensifier to *servare*, Latin for "to keep safe." Conservatives, then, are people deeply concerned with preserving, with keeping safe. I go on from there: because they know things worthy of safekeeping; the implication here is that there might be a kind of conservatism attached to unworthy preservation, or to holding on for the sake of holding on. To some degree, holdouts are, as I've said, to be respected, first, because it is the way of the world that what goes round comes round and what seems retrograde this day may be progressive another day. But more important, these folks try to protect stability, and without stability the soul goes blindly shallow with anxious hustle, and the imagination fails in the face of a life oscillating between fast-forward and rewind. That is not to deny that being dug in can also be grave-like and suffer its own obliviousness. Some kinds of conservatives can only chant destructive slogans; the living sense is gone; reactionary movements are the clattering dance of the dead.

The bridge, a long one, between past and present is memory—the memory bridge is a figure for my more literal claim above, that memory is all the past there *is*. Along this long bridge, some of the past worth saving may, by a misapplication of the memory-mode called memorizing, be turned into sallow ghosts, thence into petrified effigies; the latter particularly in our public or external memory. Similarly, moving thoughts can become rigid abstractions (as in philosophy textbooks that trade in "isms," idealism, realism, rationalism, empiricism, etc., etc.). Poignant visions can become inert abridgments (as in those infamous Study Notes students don't admit to using.[6] This whole educational cemetery is laid out, I think, according to misguided notions concerning the afterlife of human works, the most acute case of wrongheadedness being that so-called delivery systems are separable from their content, that the concrete specificity of the original texts (in which I include responsible translations) is not inextricably involved in what is said, and that our students' fictional or philosophical imagination can be aroused by informational abstractions. Derivatives are not only failure-prone in finance.

So now to that *imagination* itself. It is a power and has products. Our souls imagine and bring about works, works of two sorts, mental imagery and external images. Most external images, verbal, visual, even auditory are—the ins and outs of this would be worthy of a big book—imitations of interior imagery, although some external images have no internal originals. (Example: conceptual art; some artists [egged on by their estheticians] claim to visualize only as they are drawing, that is, *ex post facto*; so they are not imitating psychic pictures but originating manual gestures. Some people say they relish such productions.) Certain works of the imagination aid reason directly; they are spatializations of ideas.[7]

There is behind this account of the imagination a deeper view of the soul, called "epistemological," that is, "giving an account of knowledge." In this account, which has ancient and modern versions, imagination has a Hermes-like function. (Hermes, recall, is the conductor-god who transfers souls from earth to the underworld.) Thus the imagination takes delivery from the senses, which give us the world in its solidity and gravity, and rarifies their content into transparent weightless images (sometimes taking these even further down to the mere schemata, the idea-diagrams just mentioned) until they are fit to be presented to the intellect— de-materialized, quasi-spatial presences, on which the mind can think, or in neuro-speak, which the brain can further process.

Images themselves have a wonderful ontology, mentioned above and implied in my description of image-formation. They *are* and *are not* what they represent. Pull a picture from your wallet and say, "That's my grandson." If I responded, "No, it isn't," I'd be infuriating, but I wouldn't be wrong. For an analysis of image-nature yields that very melding of Being and Non-being which so attracts and astounds the intellect attempting to think comprehensively: An image is a present absence—or an absent presence. It is a mystery of disincarnation, of which the willing mind, cunningly compromising its logical requirements, just manages to take hold.[8] (Cognitive science and neuroscience provide explanations of mental imagery that are more sharp-edged but less illuminating in my context.)

Memory, the imaginative conservative's special domain (since, as I claimed above, it makes the past have being and the present vitality), is the imagination's supply house and also workspace, for imaginative material is, I would say, basically memorial; who can imagine anything, even a futuristic prospect, that is not a modification of the past?

The imagination, then, is the worker within this memorial store; it transmutes, transfigures, and transforms memories. Sometimes it falsifies, but I think that in its invention it is less liar than interpreter. I'll put it this way: the well-conditioned imagination is a myth-recalling and myth-making imagination. It puts a background of meaning to present experience. Human meaningfulness almost always has, I think, a sense of depth to it, which in memorial space acquires the feel of "out of the past."

So it's time to meditate on the *sources* of memory. There are basic external origins, of course, sensory experiences and their evaluations—reality-derived memories. Among these are *external* images, crafted by painters and other visual artists or developed by cameras and other recording devices, snapshot-style or posed, unretouched or doctored, intended as honest testimony or passed out with a deceitful agenda—true or lying *imitations*.

And then there are *internal* images, imaginative images, effects of the productive imagination working on its psychic material. And these images of the soul raise the most acutely wonderful of all questions concerning the imagination: What are the *originals* of imaginative images? Whence comes the material that the working imagination contributes on its own, drawing on *presences* beyond those found in experiential, this-worldly memory? Most quasi-sensory elements of inner images must, for such as we are, indeed be world-derived. But there are beings, events, atmospheres that have never yet eventuated in this world, or at least were never within our sensory reach. When poets and novelists make them external for us (and we in turn internalize them) we call them fictions, but falsely, because we may find them more actual than merely real facts.

The question concerning the originals of imaginative images is, I think, ultimately theological. Explanations in terms of the sub- or unconscious are subterfuges—no one can actually locate these limbos; explaining away is not explaining. When I say "theological," I have in mind the Muses who live on Olympus and are invoked by poets from Homer to Milton, who both had access to the realm of divinity, where the Muses are quartered. So also, great novelists express, more prosaically, some sense of being visited from Beyond. And it is no accident that the greatest phenomenologist (that is, an account-giver of inner appearances, in this case of memory and imagination, in his *Confessions*) was also among the greatest theologians, namely Augustine of Hippo (354–430). In sum, the originals of memories are mostly external and come to us largely through the frontal doors of perception, but the originals of the imagination on its own are imparted—who knows whence?—to some hinterland of the soul—which, once again, it's no use to call the unconscious, for if it's just neural, how does it issue as "conscious," and if it's conscious, how is it "un"?

So much for the *ontology*, *activity*, *sources*, and *originals* of the imagination; as I said, a culpably condensed treatment worth a big book.[9] And now, one last time: Why is the imagination a specifically conservative concern so that it is rightly attached adjectivally to the noun "conservative"?

The imagination should be anybody's interest, a common interest, for just as articulateness damps rage, so imaginativeness relieves alienation. Thus, as the preservation of expressive (non-twittering) language should be a social concern, the saving of the imagination should be everyone's care. I will argue below for the implication that nothing matters more to our psychological security than the protection of children from degraded speech and vulgarized images.

What are the dangers? First, the outsourcing of the imagination, the riffing, as it were, of the in-house working imagination, to be replaced by the inundating hyper-productivity of an industrial image-source. Next, the loss of worldly originals, particularly the paving over of nature, the systematic replacement of what is given to us, is of slow growth, is deep and mysterious, by what is made by us, is quickly produced, and is complex and so completely analyzable—without being at all understood. The practical business of resisting the transmogrification of first into second nature belongs to those uncomfortable kin of conservatives, the conservationists; they are lately learning not to ride rough-shod over people's livelihoods in their enthusiasm and to find mutually satisfactory accommodations, so that conservation can become a win-win game—in the conservative mode, one might say, chuckling.

A final slew of dangers I can think of is the contraction of physical vision into the field of a miniscule window, where occurs "texting" with its digital modes: literal fingering, calculational figuring, verbal frittering. Concurrently, imaginative envisioning is overwhelmed by image-inundation, and keen intellectual appetite is spoiled by a surfeit of information.[10]

But then, what's all this to the imaginative conservative in particular? Well, we ought to be glad and close observers of all givenness, green nature above all, great sniffers-out of the corrosive vapors issuing from the excessive ingestion of the original world, the world that is, for faith, God's creation, or for philosophy, Being's appearance. Another way to put it: Imaginative conservatism means, to me at least, a grounded flexibility functioning between ideal and real, the imaginative space in which concrete specificity and universal essentiality meet—the twice-lived world, once in experienced fact and again in imaginative reflection.

Twelfth: Eccentric Centrality

Finally, an imaginative conservative will have, against all odds, an abiding faith in *eccentric centrality*. A nun I used to know once explained to me that the energy which moves the world has its center in out-of-the-way places, remote from the mere epicenters of secular power. I agree. The spirit lives in the sticks, in backwaters, small towns, in self-sufficiently recalcitrant, contentedly unregarded places, in local orchestras, neighborhood groceries, in libraries that still have books on shelves—not multiple copies of best-sellers but accumulated collections of middlingly good novels—and, above all, in face-to-face schools that transmit the tradition, its treasures of beauty and of reflection. Of course, they all must scramble, accommodate themselves to "current conditions"—a potently polymorphous notion, the correct discerning of which takes more practical wisdom than most of us possess. Thus the imaginative conservative's practical project is survival without loss of soul.

So that's the imaginative conservative I'm willing to own up to being—call it "modified Burkean," if it's better off with a label.[11] Do I then have "the Conservative Mind"? I hope not. A mind-set is a major liability for a person wanting to be thoughtful—and a premature fixative of imaginative reflection to boot.

In fact, it is legitimate history to claim that an imaginative—let it be said, a Burkean—conservative is apt to be politically a classical Liberal in the nineteenth-century English sense: of Lockean ancestry, believing in the ultimacy of individuals over groups; ready to trust elected representatives with projects for political reform but resistant to administrative compulsions of social justice; attached to private associations as loci of excellence; and, above all, cherishing liberty over the forcible equality of ideological egalitarianism—as opposed to the equality grounded in our common nature or creation. This is the merest sketch of a politics that seems to me compatible with imaginative conservatism.

My first and last care, however, is not politics (a late-learned duty) but education (an abiding passion). Education seems to me inherently conservative, being the transmission, and thus the saving, of a tradition's treasures of fiction and thought. (I can't think that the desperately "innovative" gimmickry which diverts attention from contents to delivery systems is able to reconstitute failing communities of learning.)

But education is also inherently imaginative, because from pre-school to graduate school, it consists, or should consist, primarily of learning to read books (in whatever format), books of words, symbols, diagrams, musical notes. For entry into all of these, but perhaps books of words above all, imagination is indispensable. Great poetry requires visualization to be interpretable; the word has to become a vision to be realized. (Specific example, perhaps the greatest moment of any: at the climax of the *Iliad*, Achilles is searching for the vulnerable spot in Hector's armor-encased body. The armor Hector is wearing is the suit he has stripped from the body of Patroclus, the friend of Achilles' heart, whom Achilles has sent heedlessly into battle to fight in his stead, clothed in his own armor. Now he drives his spear into Hector's gullet. Whom is he killing? Homer is silent. See it and shudder.)

Similarly, works of reflection require a kind of reverse imagination, since practically all speech about non-physical being is by bodily metaphor: The transfiguration, the transcending, of such philosophical figures is practically the same as thinking reflectively. (A not so very specific example, but perhaps among the grandest: Hegel tells of the Spirit coming into time, of God entering the world, through a "gallery of figures," human incarnations, even identifiable as historical individuals. But, he says, that's not how we are to understand his *Phenomenology of Spirit*, his account of the phenomena by which divinity becomes manifest in the world; he is not presenting imagined figures but incarnate truths. It is the most hellishly difficult but most rewarding of image-interpretations known to me; it requires ascending from visualizable images to purely thinkable originals.)

That's imaginative conservatism for a college and its students, my particular venue and charge. But what matters *most* is, as I must repeat, the education of *children*. Looking at them from the vantage point of their future teacher, I would wish this for us: that their memories be stocked with the finest products of the tradition and their minds be—gently—turned toward the outside in close looking and articulate verbalizing and toward the inside in absorbed reading and ready visualizing. Just forget for a while about "preparing them for tomorrow" and "for being productive members of today's society"—all that routine drivel deserves scare quotes since it's meant to turn us into sacrificial victims on the altar of utility. It doesn't work anyhow, since tomorrow is anybody's guess and actual producing may be by then passé. And while I'm at it: Teach children mathematics for what it is, not dreary, opaquely operational formulas, but the most immediately intelligible language in which Nature speaks to us—and the spare armature of our vision-invested imagination.

All of this can happen if schools for all ages stay resolutely *local* in place and go expansively *cosmopolitan* in time. I mean that they should preserve themselves as face-to-face communities in particular places, but dedicate themselves to absorbing living heritage from any time. For the present is too thin to live on, and the future too inexistent.

Notes

1. "Simulacrum" because "conservative" practically *means* "moderate"—or should. I'm speaking here of an obtusely aggressive public persona, not of the understandably aggrieved

human souls who have donned it; in some respects I sympathize with them.

2. In an essay the claim to candor will, I hope, carry some credit; in politics "quite candidly" is a discrediting speech-tic.

3. There is a seriously absurd notion abroad that wise planning is based on the whole informational apparatus that results from non-reflective mentation: "big" data, facts, number-crunchings, etc. My experience says that in practical judgments concerning life everything that matters—purposes above all, but also limits of tolerable deviation and of acceptable means—will have been predetermined by engaged pondering. *Then* you go fact-finding, either to help you bully colleagues or to persuade you it's not worth the battle—but no one who has not once simply overridden the experts—well, I won't go there.

   Moreover, stuff yields information and facts are found only within a given referential framework.

4. *Theses on Feuerbach XI*: "The philosophers have only interpreted the world; the point is to *change* it."

5. African Methodist Episcopal Church.

6. Though they too have a place—as indexes to very long novels.

7. Such as logical and mathematical diagrams, which appear, it seems, in a blank internal imaginative field in which reason—how is a mystery—can inscribe its structures. There are, of course, also external images produced by nature, such as reflections.

8. I want to distinguish sharply the *Non-being constitutionally inherent* in both real and imagined images from *virtuality*, which is a *discretionary mode* of reception, hence, as I said, a danger. More accurately, virtuality is an environment, "the virtual world." When the promise of this virtual world to come is fulfilled, it will divorce its—presumably still voluntary—participants pretty finally (if only in stretches) from the physical world; they will be cocooned in a world-simulacrum that is absolutely immediate, without intervening organs of sensation or physical distances—achieved by direct electronic stimulation of the brain that subserves our perceptions. It will be a complete environment, a replacement world, with-

out reality-resistance and therefore completely manipulable—by the individual for his own pleasure or by the technological provider with alien motives: inactuality as world-principle—otherwise put, an image-world humanly contrived without originals. Here the wondrous element of Non-being is turned against the very images it sustained *as* images, caused to *be* images; in the virtual world, not only have mental images cast loose from originals, but instead of being within us, we are within them, as in a super-mind.

As Milton's Satan says, "The mind is its own place, and in itself / Can make a Heaven of Hell, a Hell of Heaven." Hell, I would think. In sum, virtuality is a term from the devil's dictionary, a good word, "virtue," gone ambiguous as in "virtual reality," potently unreal reality. Conservationists of the imagination should think twice. This term has suction power.

9. See E. Brann, *The World of the Imagination* (1991).

10. Here is an omen: The number of visitors to our national parks is on a downward trend; the reason given is in a headline: "Why go outside when you have an iPhone?" (*Economist*, August 17, 2013).

11. Here's what's "Burkean": Edmund Burke (1729–97) is for reform that is not ideologically driven; he is radical when reason-sustained popular opinion requires it (Burke was a supporter of our Revolution); he's for minimum moralism and conciliatory politics out of respect for tradition and care for stability; he pays deference both to nature and historical conditions; he supports incremental change and the narrowest tailoring of planned interventions. He's *not* for philosophy, mistaking it, I think, for rationalism (or maybe just being an Englishman of a traditional cast of mind)—that's where my revisionism comes in: I'm for Burke *plus* philosophy. And certainly, if conservatives may, on occasion, be divided into Burkeans and bullies, I'll declare for the former.